Knowing God's Will — and Doing It!

Knowing
God's Will —
and Doing It!

by

J. Grant Howard, Jr.

ZONDERVAN
PUBLISHING HOUSE
OF THE ZONDERVAN CORPORATION
GRAND RAPIDS, MICHIGAN 49506

KNOWING GOD'S WILL — AND DOING IT!
Copyright © 1976 by The Zondervan Corporation
Grand Rapids, Michigan

Library of Congress Cataloging in Publication Data

Howard, J.   Grant.
    Knowing God's will — and doing it!

    1.   God—Will.   2.   Christian life—1960-
I.   Title.
BV4501.2.H627   248'.4   75-42141

ISBN 0-310-26281-X

All Scripture quotations are from *The New American Standard Bible.* Copyright ©
1960, 1962, 1963, 1968, 1971 by the Lockman Foundation. Printed by Creation
House. Grateful acknowledgment is made to the Lockman Foundation for permission
to use this material.

Printed in the United States of America

83 84 85 86 87 88 — 15 14 13 12 11 10

To Dad and Mom

who have provided

a beautiful context

for me to discover and

do the will of God

Contents

Preface

Introduction

1. Two Aspects of the Will of God   15
2. The Desired Will of God for All Individuals   23
3. The Will of God in the Word of God   27
4. Discovering and Doing the Will of God   33
5. Processing the Data Properly   41
6. The Will of God and Your World   47
7. Circumstances and the Will of God   53
8. Counsel and the Will of God   61
9. Conscience and the Will of God   67
10. Common Sense and the Will of God   73
11. Compulsion and the Will of God   79
12. Contentment and the Will of God   83
13. Suppose I Don't Do the Will of God   91
14. Questions About the Will of God   101
15. Putting It All Together   113

Preface

The main purpose of this book is to examine the concept of the will of God from a biblical perspective and to develop some of the practical implications of the scriptural teachings concerning it. The presentation is popular rather than technical; practical rather than theoretical.

I am indebted to the members of the Camelback Bible Church in Phoenix, Arizona, who allowed me as their pastor for nine years the privilege of studying and sharing with them many of these concepts in embryonic form. Along the way, many other groups and individuals have helped to revise and refine my thinking on this topic. I am grateful to Western Conservative Baptist Seminary for time off in the summers of 1974 and 1975 to collect, arrange, and write these thoughts in a form that I trust will be palatable and profitable for all who read them. This is obviously not the final word on the will of God. Who can pronounce the final word on anything that has to do with God? Hopefully, it will be used to stimulate many to think about and live in His will.

J. GRANT HOWARD, JR.

Welcome to this book! How did you happen to get hold of it? Browsing in a bookstore? Sent away for it? Borrowed it? Someone gave it to you? Well, no matter how you secured it, it's obvious that you now have it, and I hope you are going to read it. Now, before you go any further, let me ask you one basic question:

Is it God's will for you to read this book?

It's really not fair to put you on the spot like this, is it? After all, you got the book to find out about the will of God, and on the first page the author wants you to come up with an answer that requires a profound understanding of the subject. Okay, I'll tell you what, we won't press the issue any more right now. But keep the question in mind as you read, because the pages that lie ahead are designed to furnish you with the information you need to answer it with confidence.

1

Two Aspects of the Will of God

Any discussion of the will of God that is biblically oriented must, of necessity, take into account all that the Bible reveals about the subject. Since this is not a technical treatment, we will not look at every Old Testament and New Testament reference referring directly or indirectly to the will of God — there are many of them. We will, instead, focus our attention on certain, selected key passages of Scripture that crystallize for us the basic teaching of the rest of the Bible on this important subject.

One of the most essential things we need to know about the will of God is that the Bible gives this concept — "the will of God" — two distinct and different meanings. It is imperative that we know what they are and that we understand both the distinctions and the relationship between them. So we begin our study by defining and describing the two aspects of the will of God.

The determined will of God

Scripture teaches us that God has a predetermined plan for every life. It is that which *will happen*. It is inevitable, unconditional, immutable, irresistible, comprehensive, and purposeful.

It is also, for the most part, unpredictable. It includes everything — even sin and suffering. It involves everything — even human responsibility and human decisions.

Ephesians 1:11 says that God "works all things after the counsel of His will." This underscores God's sovereign involvement in everything. He is at work in every life and in every area of life. He counsels with no one else. He does it all on His own. He does not react to situations; He creates them. The verb "works" is in the present tense, indicating that God is in charge at all times. He does not get things started and then let them go on their own. He is consistently, actively involved in our world and in our lives. Everything that happens, happens within the determined will of God. Ephesians 1:11 makes this clear.

God's attitude toward His activity is seen in Ephesians 1:5 — "the kind intention of His will" (cf. v. 9). The word for "kind intention" literally means "good pleasure." He does things in a certain way because it pleases Him. God is not a passive or even a neutral administrator. Verse 9 tells us there is mystery in His will. Obviously, there is immense mystery in both the what and the why of His sovereign plan. We are allowed to understand it only to the degree He chooses to reveal it to us. What is the ultimate purpose for God's doing things the way He wants to do them? Verses 6, 12, and 14 answer this — to bring glory to Himself.

We cannot always understand and often find it difficult to accept the things that do happen, but we can rest assured that everything ultimately brings glory to God (cf. Isa. 42:8; John 17:4, 5; 1 Peter 4:11).

A specific instance of the determined will of God is found in Ephesians 1:1, "Paul, an apostle of Christ Jesus by the will of God." Being an apostle was something God had determined would happen in the life of Paul. The fact that His will is irresistible is seen in Romans 9:19 when the question is asked: "For who resists His will?" The answer implied is "No one." Romans 9:6-29, the context of this passage, underscores the fact that God has a sovereign plan that is operating in everyone's life. Is God's determined will fixed or does He find it necessary to make mid-course corrections now and then? Hebrews 6:17 reveals that His purpose is unchangeable and that this is confirmed by His own divine oath.

So when we talk about the will of God, we must realize that there is more than one aspect to it. The *determined* will of God is the comprehensive, eternal plan that God has decided to put into operation in the world in general and in your life in particular.

Within the context of this divine plan, sin occurs. This raises two basic questions. First, was sin really a part of *God's* plan? The Bible says yes, for God's *eternal* plan included the sacrifice of Christ on the cross for *sinful* man (1 Peter 1:18-20; Eph. 1:4, 5). Sin was not an unexpected intrusion; it was a part of the plan designed by God. Second, doesn't this make God responsible for sin? The Bible says no. The Bible never blames God for sin. Man, exercising his genuine free will, is always held responsible for committing sin (Rom. 3:9-23). Within the context of God's sovereign holiness there exists the reality of man's responsible sinfulness. To us, these two sets of facts appear contradictory, yet they are both clearly revealed as true in Scripture. So we should regard the contradictions as *apparent* rather than real. In the mind of an omniscient God they are resolved.

Why is sin a part of God's plan at all? At least one reason is clear. Because sin exists, God can show forth His glory not only as the Creator of all things but also as the Redeemer of all things.

Can I know the determined will of God for my life? *Yes — after it has occurred!* You now know that God's determined will for your life was that you be born of certain parents, in a certain location, under certain conditions, and that you be male or female. You now know that God determined for you to have certain features, certain experiences, certain teachers, certain interests, certain friends, a certain kind of education, and certain brothers and/or sisters, or perhaps to be an only child. In other words, everything that has happened in your life to this moment has been part of God's determined will for your life. It has

17

happened because He has determined it to be so.

What about the future? Can I know any part of God's determined will for my life in the future? Your spiritual position and eternal destiny are the only two things you can know with certainty. If you are *in Christ* now, you can know for certain that you will remain in Christ at every moment in the future (John 5:24; 10:27-29; Rom. 5:1; 2 Cor. 5:17). If you are not a Christian, you are *in sin* right now and you can know for certain that you will remain in that spiritually dead position in the future unless and until you personally receive Christ as your Savior (Eph. 2:1-3). Furthermore, the one in Christ can know for certain his eternal destiny — heaven (John 14:1-3; 2 Cor. 5:6-8; 1 Thess. 4:13-18). The one in sin can know for certain his eternal destiny — hell — if he remains in sin (John 3:36; 5:29).

The remainder of your future is hidden from you until it happens. Your career, marriage partner, home location, grades in school, friends, sicknesses, accidents, honors, travels, income, retirement, etc., are all part of God's determined will but are not revealed to you ahead of time. Apart from your spiritual position and eternal destiny, all that will happen in your life cannot be predicted with absolute certainty.

What about God's determined will for the world in general? All the events of past history have happened and thus we now know they were a part of God's determined will. Do we know anything about God's plan in days to come? The Bible reveals events that will take place in the future, such as the coming of Christ, the various judgments, the great tribulation, the rise of Antichrist, the new heavens and the new earth, etc. These we know for certain will take place, because God has told us they will. But many, many things other than those predicted in the Word of God will happen, for they have been determined by the God of the Word. Wars will be fought, governments will be overthrown, planes will crash, inventions will take place, teams will win games, crops will be harvested — but only God knows for certain when and where and why. I don't know whether it is

God's determined will that this book be published. If you are reading it, it was!

What should be the Christian's attitude toward the determined will of God? He should recognize it as a reality — clearly taught in the Word of God. Rest in it as good, because that's what God says about it — He causes all things to work together for good to those who love Him (Rom. 8:28). Beyond that, don't worry about it and don't try to figure it out, because His ways are unfathomable (Rom. 11:33).

The desired will of God

Another aspect of the will of God is His desired will. The determined will is that which will happen. The desired will is that which he *wants to happen* in every person's life. It is not inevitable. It may or may not happen. It is not unconditional. It is based on our decisions. It is not irresistible. We can choose not to do it. And most significant, it is not a mystery. It is something we can know and should do.

In Acts 20:27 Paul reminds the Ephesian leaders that while he had been with them he declared to them the whole purpose of God. "Purpose" can also be translated "counsel," or "intentions." Paul told them what God intended for them to be and do. He taught them all about God's desired will for their lives. So here is an aspect of the will of God that can be known and can be communicated from person to person. Paul's prayer for the Colossian believers was "that you may be filled with the knowledge of His will in all spiritual wisdom and understanding, so that you may walk in a manner worthy of the Lord" (1:9, 10). The will of God was something they could understand and put into practice. Believers are instructed to be transformed by the renewing of their minds so that they can "prove what the will of God is" (Rom. 12:2). To "prove" refers to the process of testing and analyzing. The will of God is something we discover — with minds renewed by the Word of God. Christians are exhorted to "understand what the will of the Lord is" (Eph. 5:17). The Greek word translated "understand" means "to put together." Discovering the will of God is a process of putting together data

19

from His Word and from His world. Hebrews 13:20, 21 states that it is God who can "equip you in every good thing to do His will."

These verses show us that there is an aspect of the will of God that we can know and do. When we talk about discovering and about doing the will of God, it is this aspect that we refer to. The will of God is not something deep and mysterious that can be discovered only by certain people in certain situations. Any believer can know it and do it. It is simply and yet profoundly what God wants to happen in your life.

The relation between the determined will and the desired will of God

The determined will of God is that which will happen. The desired will of God is that which God wants to happen. We do not know what will happen but we do know what He wants to happen. Ephesians 5:25 clearly reveals one aspect of the desired will of God for me. I am to love my wife. I am to love her as Christ loves the church — by acting to meet her needs. Suppose she needs help in caring for the children, but I'm tired and tied to a television program and so I fail to act to meet her needs; I fail to love her. I am out of the desired will of God, because I have failed to do what I know He wants me to do in terms of my relationship to my wife at that moment. That failure is sin. It affects my fellowship with God and with my wife. I need to remedy the situation by admitting my failure and confessing it to the persons who have been wronged. Why? Because that procedure is also a part of God's desired will for me when I go astray (James 5:16; 1 John 1:9).

How does all of this relate to His determined will? My failure to love my wife properly on that occasion was, somehow, a part of God's determined will for my life. It was one of the many details God included in His program for my life. But even though it was part of *His program*, it was *my problem*. I was responsible for my failure to act lovingly. I had to face that fact and act to bring things back into their proper relationship.

Tonight my wife said she was fixing waffles for supper and that she was mentally preparing herself to cope with the situation if the waffles stuck to the waffle iron. They did. Badly. After chiseling two burnt waffles off the irons, we gave up and borrowed a neighbor's. It was the determined will of God that the waffles stick. It was the desired will of God that Audrey experience peace in the midst of pressure (John 16:33). She did. She was "in the will of God."

We are always in God's determined will — His plan. His determined will involves certainty without compulsion. That is, it must happen and it will happen, but without our feeling that we are being forced or manipulated to accomplish it. We sense a freedom to do what we want to do, and that freedom to decide and act is very real and quite genuine, but it exists and is exercised within the context of God's sovereignly determined plan. With our finite minds we cannot explain how this could be true. We must simply accept the fact that the Word of God says it is.

Though we are always in God's determined will (His plan), we may or may not be in His desired will (His pleasure).

The rest of this book will deal with the desired will of God — that which God wants to happen in the life of every person. We will look at what it is in general, then in particular, and find out how we discover it and how we do it.

2

The Desired Will of God for All Individuals

For the unsaved

What does God want to happen in the life of the unsaved? First Timothy 2:4 says that God "desires all men to be saved and to come to the knowledge of the truth." This is His desired will rather than his determined will, since not all will be saved. The "whosoevers" in passages like John 3:16 and Romans 10:13 are universal in their appeal, further supporting the fact that God wants every person to be saved. Many reject Christ, however, and remain lost. This is part of the determined will of God, or in more theological terms, it is the biblical doctrine of election or predestination, which also involves, negatively, those who are not saved. No one knows who the elect are; therefore, we don't know the determined will of God with reference to the salvation of any individual. We do know the desired will of God for all individuals and thus our responsibility is to preach the gospel to every creature. Anyone who wants to be saved and exercises his conscious, deliberate choice to accept Christ will be saved. Anyone who doesn't want to be saved and exercises his conscious, deliberate choice to reject Christ will be lost. Nobody will be saved against his own will. Nobody will be lost apart from his own will.

The Christian knows the will of God for every unsaved person — that he or she be saved. You could tap an unsaved person on the shoulder any place in the world and say to him, "I know God's will for your life. It is that you be saved!"

For the saved

You could also tap any believer on the shoulder and say to him: "I know God's will for your life. You are to be sanctified." Christians are given instructions to this effect in 1 Thessalonians 4:1-7:

> Finally then, brethren, we request and exhort you in the Lord Jesus that, as you received from us instruction as to how you ought to walk and please God (just as you actually do walk), that you may excel still more. For you know what commandments we gave you by the authority of the Lord Jesus. For this is the will of God, your sanctification; that is, that you abstain from sexual immorality (1 Thess. 4:1-3).

In verse 1 believers are exhorted to excel more and more in a way of life that is pleasing to God. Verse 2 indicates that this is to be based on obedience to the commandments that came from the Lord. A summary explanatory statement is given in verse 3: "For this is the will of God, your sanctification." From the preceding verses we see that sanctification is growing in a walk pleasing to God. In the latter part of verse 3 sanctification is particularized as sexual purity — one key aspect of a walk pleasing to God. Sanctification is what God wants to happen in the life of the believer. Sanctification means "to be set apart." The believer is set apart to love and to serve God. This involves holiness. Growth is the process of change toward more holiness in one's life. This is the will of God for every believer.

Growth follows birth in the natural realm. So it does in the spiritual realm. In both realms growth takes place in the specific details of life over a period of time. Thus, sanctification is personal, practical, and progressive.

In many places in the Bible the phrase "will of God" is used in reference to some personal, practical aspect of sanctification. We have seen in 1 Thessalonians 4:3 that it is related specifically to sexual purity. In 1 Thessalonians 5:16-18 the three impera- tives "rejoice," "pray," and "give thanks" are all said to be the will of God for the believer. These are activities that God wants to happen in the lives of Christians. If I'm not rejoicing, praying, and filled with thankfulness, then I'm out of the will of God.

First Peter 4:1, 2 relates the will of God to suffering. Verse 1 teaches us that Christ went through the suffering of life and death with the mental attitude that such was the will of His Father and He was committed to it. With the same mental attitude, the believer can go through suffering without going to pieces and sinning. With such an attitude, the believer can live life not for the lusts of men but for the will of God. The will of God is the opposite of the lusts of men. One is human; the other divine. When you are in the will of God, the world may malign you (v. 4) and you may suffer as a result, but even that is a part of the will of God. A key point in the passage: the will of God is something we live; it may involve suffering but it ought not to involve sin.

First Peter 4:19 reiterates this concept of suffering *accord- ing to the will of God.* Keep doing the right thing and if in so doing you suffer, you suffer according to the will of God. Sub- mission to the ordinances of men is required of every believer (1 Peter 2:15). Why? Because it is the will of God. Slaves are told to be obedient to their masters and to render their service with honest sincerity as to Christ (Eph. 6:5-8). When you function like this, you will be doing the will of God from the heart. The will of God involves proper actions that stem from right motives.

Note how personal and practical the will of God is for the Christian. It is linked directly to such activities as living in sexual purity, rejoicing, praying, suffering, submitting, and serving — all things the Christian *does.* The verb "to do" is significantly present in numerous New Testament references to the will of God: "Thy will be *done* on earth" (Matt. 6:10); ". . . he who does the will of My Father" (Matt. 7:21); "if anyone is God-fearing, and *does* His will . . ." (John 9:31); "David . . . a man after My heart, who will *do* all My will" (Acts 13:22). The point is patently clear. The believer must not sit back and wait for the will of God to take place in his life. He must become actively involved in *doing* the will of God. The relationship of Christ to the will of the Father is certainly illustrative of this. He told His disciples that He was totally committed to doing the will of His Father (John 4:34). He informed the Pharisees: "I always do the things that are pleasing to Him" (John 8:29). For Christ the determined and the desired will of the Father were one and the same; even so, He went through the process of choosing to do the will of God. It was not always a simple, automatic decision, for in the Garden of Gethsemane He said, "Father, if Thou art willing, remove this cup from Me; yet not My will, but Thine be done" (Luke 22:42). He struggled with the issues and chose to do the will of God. That is why He can intercede sympathetically for us today at the right hand of the Father as we struggle with decisions to do the will of God (Heb. 4:14-16). That is also why the writer of Hebrews could promise that God, through Jesus Christ, would equip believers in every good thing to do His will (13:20, 21).

The desired will of God for the believer is to be sanctified — to grow and mature into increasing Christlikeness. Sanctification embraces every area of life. This means that the words a young suitor chooses to speak are just as much a part of the will of God as the woman he chooses to marry. Sanctification involves knowing the Word and doing it by the power of the Holy Spirit. That leads us to consider the place of the Word of God in the will of God.

3

The Will of God in the Word of God

The purpose of the Word

Second Timothy 3:16, 17 deals explicitly with the purpose of the Word of God:

> All Scripture is inspired by God and profitable for teaching, for reproof, for correction, for training in righteousness; that the man of God may be adequate, equipped for every good work.

First the origin is clearly stated: all Scripture is inspired by God. "Inspired by God" could be more literally translated "God-breathed." When you breathe on a cold window, you see condensation. The condensation came from your warm breath. In a unique way the Scriptures came from God. They are the result of His "breathing out" a revelation to us. This is the doctrine of inspiration and it simply means that the ultimate source of all Scripture is God.

Because of its divine source, Scripture has a significant and unique use. It is beneficial and useful in four specific spheres. It is profitable for teaching — the activity of imparting truth; for reproof — the activity of convincing and convicting one of error in thought or conduct; for correction — the activity of restoring one to the right place and path; and for training in righteousness — the entire process of education from instruction to chastisement. This summary of the profitable use of Scripture can be viewed as four facets to be brought to bear in the believer's life. It is also possible that there is a planned sequence in this list. Teaching is the presentation of the gospel to the unsaved, reproof is the convicting work of the Spirit, correction is the work of conversion, and instruction in righteousness is the process of growth.

The ultimate objective or purpose is stated in verse 17 — that the man of God may be *adequate.* "Adequate" is the translation of the Greek word *artios*, which means "that which is right, proper, and suitable." The next word in the verse — *equipped* — is an intensified form (*exartizo*) of the same Greek word and means "to be thoroughly equipped." What do we often do to emphasize a point? We restate it, saying the same word louder or adding a word for emphasis. Paul couldn't write louder but he could restate the same word and add to it for emphasis. This is precisely what he did. He said, in effect, "The Word of God is designed to *equip* the man of God — did you get that? — I mean to *thoroughly equip* him!" Thoroughly equip him to do what? To engage in every good work. "Every good work" is nothing more nor less than the *will of God!* Ephesians 2:10 reinforces the concept that the believer is saved for this specific purpose: "For we are His workmanship, created in Christ Jesus for good works, which God prepared beforehand, that we should walk in them." "Good works" is another way of referring to the will of God.

Thus the ultimate purpose of the Word of God in my life is to equip me to do the will of God. The primary revelation of the will of God for my life is in the Word of God. I cannot know God's will apart from His Word. Other passages state this same concept in different ways. Romans 12:2 says that we are transformed by the renewing of our minds so that we can prove what the will of God is. As the mind is furnished with the Word, it is more and more capable of discovering the will of God. Hebrews 5:14 indicates that as we take in the solid food (of the Word) and train ourselves to apply it, we can discern good and evil and so know the will of God. Titus 2:11, 12 reveals that the grace of God has appeared, bringing salvation to all, and is instructing us (by the Word) to renounce ungodliness and worldly desires and to live sensibly, righteously, and godly — i.e., to do the will of God — in the present age.

Peter puts it this way: "Like newborn babes, long for the pure milk of the word, that by it you may grow in respect to salvation [doing the will of God]" (1 Peter 2:2).

The precepts of the Word

Precepts are specific, detailed instructions as to what God wants the believer to do and not to do. They tell him what is right and what is wrong. For example, the Word makes it clear that it is *right* to pray, to assemble, to grow, to trust, to cast our cares on God, to witness, to submit to one another, to confess, to love, to admonish, to obey, to forgive, etc. The Word also makes it plain that it is *wrong* to lie, to cheat, to steal, to murder, to commit adultery, to commit idolatry, to gossip, to covet, to yield to temptation, etc. These precepts and many others like them are presented in both the Old and the New Testaments at numerous times and in numerous ways and give us explicit revelation of the will of God for every believer.

The normal experience of incoming high school freshmen is to receive a student handbook. Such a handbook contains all the rules and regulations for the students. It tells them what they may do and what they may not do. The pages are filled with specific, detailed directions regarding the will of the school administration for the student. They are not recommendations or suggestions. They are precepts to be obeyed.

In the same manner, God has given every believer a handbook with many of the basic rules and regulations for life. If and when a believer follows these rules, he is in the will of God. When he consciously violates them, he is out of the will of God.

Therefore I must know the precepts taught in the Word if I am going to do the will of God.

The principles of the Word

Principles are general directions that must be applied to specific situations. The sign that reads "SPEED LIMIT 25 MPH" is a precept. The sign that reads "DRIVE CAREFULLY" is a principle. I apply the latter in one way in heavy traffic and in another way on a deserted street. The Scriptures also contain principles that are valid in any society at any time. One must simply know the principle and then apply it to a given situation. For example, 2 Corinthians 6:14 says, "Do not be bound together with unbelievers." This is a biblical principle that deals with the believer's relationships. It gives the believer the will of God in terms of a general principle or guideline. Young people must apply it to their dating relationships; businessmen, to their business alliances; a housewife, to her invitation to join a social club; and a collegian, to pledging a fraternity or sorority.

Another principle is found in 1 Thessalonians 4:11, 12. Here the principle is that of *work*. The Christian is to support himself and his family in such a way that he is neither a busybody nor a beggar. If one is physically and mentally capable of working and yet is lazy and on welfare, he is in violation of this principle and is therefore out of the will of God. The necessity of work is explicit in regard to the principle, but the type and time and place of work is not mentioned.

The Word of God is filled with abiding and unchanging principles such as the above. The believer must understand them and properly apply them to his own life situations in order to discover and do the will of God.

The importance of the Word

Is the Bible the only revelation of the will of God for the believer? No, God uses other means to communicate and confirm His will to us and these will be examined in later chapters, *but the Word of God is the* primary *and* sufficient *revelation of* the will of God to the believer. We know this because we know that the person who can understand and apply the Word is thoroughly equipped to function in this world (2 Tim. 3:16, 17). The Word does not partially equip the believer. Its principles and precepts do not leave the Christian deficient in certain areas. They prepare him to do "every good work." Other factors, such as circumstances, counsel, feelings, desires, etc., are also involved in discovering and doing God's will but these are *secondary* and *supplementary* to the Word.

Does the Bible contain a complete and comprehensive revelation of the will of God for every believer? Complete — yes, in that *every area* of life is dealt with. Otherwise, the Word could not be said to *thoroughly equip* the believer. Comprehensive — no, in that *every detail* of life is dealt with in the Word. The Word does not tell us how often to eat, when to take a vacation, what TV programs to watch, or which manufactured goods to buy — but in these instances we can take biblical principles and seek to determine their implications.

Now we are ready to consider the process of getting into the Word — discovering its precepts and principles and using them to determine the will of God.

31

4

Discovering and Doing
the Will of God

Program yourself with the Word

A computer is of no value until it is programmed. It is just a big, beautiful, expensive machine loaded with potential. Program it and feed it data, and it will do more work more accurately than a multitude of people. The believer also represents tremendous potential for the Lord, but his potential cannot be realized until he begins to be programmed with the Word of God.

When we are converted, we come into the Christian life as those who have been held captive by Satan *to do his will* (2 Tim. 2:26), as those who have been used to walking "according to the course of this world, according to the prince of the power of the air, of the spirit that is now working in the sons of disobedience . . . [living] in the lusts of our flesh, indulging the desires of the flesh and of the mind . . . by nature children of wrath, even as the rest" (Eph. 2:1-3). We need to be reprogrammed! To put it in the words of Romans 12:2, we need a renewing of our minds.

This is the thrust of the teaching ministry of the Holy Spirit in the life of every believer. Predicted in John 14:26, "He will teach you all things," and John 16:13, "He will guide you into all truth," it is now that potential available to every believer. John continues to deal with this in his first Epistle where he reminds believers that they are not at the mercy of false teachers, each of them has the indwelling Holy Spirit and each and every one of them can know and understand the Word on his own (1 John 2:20). This is not to depreciate the need for and the importance of those who teach the Word but it is to make every believer aware of his capacity to study and understand the Word on his own. First John 2:27 reiterates and reinforces this concept.

A primary passage dealing with the teaching ministry of the Holy Spirit is 1 Corinthians 2:6—3:3. Verse 12 of chapter 2 tells us that the Spirit will enable us to "know" the things freely given to us by God. Verse 15 illuminates this concept with the idea that "he who is spiritual appraises all things." The "all things" refers to God's revelation to us in the Word, since it is so used numerous times in the preceding verses. "Appraise" is from the Greek word *anakrino*, which means "to investigate." It is a legal term used in extrabiblical Greek of judicial investigations and interrogations. It and its related forms are often translated "to judge" in the New Testament. The same word is used in 1 Corinthians 2:14 as a commentary on the inability of the natural (unsaved) person to accept and understand the things of the Spirit of God. He cannot accept and understand them, because they are "spiritually appraised." The person who has the Spirit is appraising all things; that is, he is consistently and capably investigating and examining the Word of God. That is what the Bereans were doing: "They received the Word with great eagerness, examining (*anakrino*) the Scriptures daily, to see whether these things were so" (Acts 17:11). Personal Bible study is the process of careful, consistent investigation into the meaning of the text. This involves more than a superficial reading or even a casual listening to someone else talk about it.

The latter part of verse 15 indicates that this kind of person cannot be investigated with accuracy by others — unless they too know the mind of the Lord (v. 16). The conclusion is summarized in the latter part of verse 16: The one who appraises all things is the one who has the mind of Christ. He is thinking like Christ. In other words, as the Spirit teaches us the Word, we begin to think like Christ.

What is the significance of the word "spiritual" in verse 15? It refers to one who is characterized by the Holy Spirit — one in whom the Holy Spirit is doing His work of teaching and transforming and through whom He is transmitting truth to others. But note specifically that the spiritual one is appraising all things; he is knowledgeable in the Word of God. That is because a knowledge of the Word is basic to transformation by, and transmission of, the truth.

Gaining knowledge takes *time*. During the time since the Corinthians had believed, they had had opportunity to become knowledgeable in the Word. Had they done so? The answer is a probing negative:

> And I, brethren, could not speak to you as to spiritual men, but as to men of flesh, as to babes in Christ. I gave you milk to drink, not solid food; for you were not yet able to receive it. Indeed, even now you are not yet able, for you are still fleshly. For since there is jealousy and strife among you, are you not fleshly, and are you not walking like mere men? (1 Cor. 3:1-3).

Paul had not been able to relate to them as spiritual people when he first met them; they were at that point babes in Christ (v. 1). He fed them milk — a diet proper for spiritual babes (v. 2a). Time passed and they were still fleshly — babes (v. 2b-3a). They were proving it by the way they acted (v. 3b). It takes time plus truth for a person to be classified as spiritual. They had put in the time but had not grasped the truth.

Do not miss the significance of the fact that "he who is spiritual *appraises* all things." To learn to appraise the Word is to take the first step in programming oneself with the Word. Can you personally on your own investigate the Word? Is your church equipping you and others to do this? Are you an active participant in an ongoing study of the Word or are you a passive recipient of somebody else's investigation of the Word? Are you able to appraise the Word independently? If you are a pastor or a Sunday school teacher, are you equipping saints to do this for themselves? Many believers have spent their whole Christian life in the spiritual dining room, feasting on what others prepared for them. We have a large, growing membership in the "Doctrinal Diners' Club." The next, natural, and necessary step is to take these members into the kitchen and let them learn how to prepare and serve spiritual meals — to themselves and to others.

When the believer gets into the Word, the Word gets into the believer! Hebrews 4:12 states that

> the Word of God is living and active and sharper than any two-edged sword, and piercing as far as the division of soul and spirit, of both joints and marrow, and able to judge the thoughts and intentions of the heart.

The impact of this truth is that the Word has such a quality to it that it pierces, penetrates, and probes our total person. It is capable of judging the thoughts and intentions of the heart. The word "judge" is from the Greek *kritikos*, from which we get our words "critic" and "critique." As we appraise the Word, the Word appraises us. We look into it; it looks into us. As we investigate it, we are investigated by it. As this process takes place, we are being internally programmed by the Word.

The only way you can be sure this takes place is to see to it that you are involved in a consistent intake of the Word of God. Part of the work of the church is to help you to do so. Every Christian ought to be identified with a local church where he can both be fed and learn how to feed himself. If you aren't presently in a church, find one that will provide this for you. If your church isn't doing this for you, talk to the leaders and make them aware of your needs.

ultimately depend upon how you are programmed.

So Paul in Romans 12:2 relates spiritual growth directly to the discovery of the will of God. As the mind is renewed, the believer becomes more qualified to examine all the facts in a life situation and discover and do the will of God.

Three words are added to the end of verse 2 to amplify what the will of God is. Possibly Paul thought the concept of the "will of God" was somewhat vague and nebulous for his readers; so he added three words to describe it. The will of God is that which is *good*. The Word gives us the standard as to what is good. If you know the Word, you will know what is good for you! Next, the will of God is that which is *acceptable* or *pleasing*. To whom? To God. The Lord used the same word when he said, "I always do the things that are pleasing to Him" (John 8:29). "Good" tends to operate in the context of what is right and what is wrong. "Pleasing" tends to operate in the context of questions such as these: "Who are those who care?" "Who will be hurt?" "Who will be made happy?" The will of God is that which is pleasing to my heavenly Father. Again I'm driven back to the Word. If I don't know what He likes, I'm not sure what the will of God is.

If it is not pleasing to God, it is disappointing to Him. Chances are if He is disappointed and displeased with my attitudes or actions, then certain significant others here on earth will react the same way; e.g., my mate, my children, my parents, and my pastor. For example, if a teenager is constantly doing that which displeases his parents, this is a good indication that he is out of the will of God. The reactions of others can be helpful indicators of God's will.

The will of God is *perfect*. This is translated from the Greek word meaning "mature" or "full-grown." The will of God is that which is grown-up, as opposed to that which is childish. When you are tempted to act like a baby, it is a good indication that you are out of the will of God. Babies pout, throw fits, want their own way, are oblivious to the needs of others, interrupt, talk back, forget, cry, etc. When a teenager throws a fit, when a husband pouts all weekend, when a woman uses tears to get her way — these are probably signs that the will of God is being sidelined for the moment. When I am in the will of God, I will be acting like a mature adult.

These three key words — *good, pleasing, perfect* — describe the nature of the will of God. When my attitudes and actions are bad, disappointing, and immature, I ought to pause and reflect; chances are I'm not using a mind programmed with the Word to evaluate data from my world to discover and do the will of God. But we need more insight on how to do this. The next chapter should provide it for us.

5

Processing the Data Properly

You are driving along the freeway late one evening in a hurry to get home. There is very little traffic and it hasn't rained in days. There are no patrol cars in sight; your car is in good shape; and your tires are brand new. The sign says "SPEED LIMIT 55 MPH." You process all of that data through your mind and then you decide whether you will stay at 55 MPH or go 65 MPH and get home sooner. What is the will of God in this matter? Well, it is clearly revealed in Romans 13:1-7 that every person is to be in subjection to the governing authorities and the one who resists this authority has opposed the ordinance of God. In this case the authorities have determined that 55 MPH is the speed limit. If you are programmed with that biblical truth, you will head for home (in the will of God) at 55 MPH. But let us say you decide to go faster and take your chances of getting caught. Or you are not paying any attention to your speed and it creeps on up to 65. In either case you are out of the will of God. The will of God is that you obey the speed limits set by the civil authorities. A lot of Christians know the facts of Romans 13:1-7, but their minds haven't really been *renewed* by these truths and their lives haven't really been *transformed* by them. They obey when it is convenient, rather than on the basis of conviction.

Incidentally, computers have consistent convictions. They don't waver when they process the data. Paul says believers are to function likewise — not automatically, but thoughtfully, with deeply imbedded, consistent, personal convictions (Rom. 14:5). A Christian adequately programmed with the concepts in Romans 13 will stay within the speed limit, regardless of what he sees in his rear-view mirror.

Bill is a new Christian who is making real progress in his spiritual growth. But he is shy and retiring and tends to keep a lot of things to himself. As a result, nobody knows much about what God is doing in his life. Bill is taking solid spiritual strides but he is a silent saint who doesn't tell anybody what's happening. There is an area of the will of God Bill needs to be made aware of. The Bible says that if one member of the body is honored (and personal growth would be a case in point), all the members are to rejoice with him (1 Cor. 12:26). How can they when they don't know what's going on in Bill's life? Again, 1 Timothy 4:15 teaches us that we are to be saturated with the Word of God and that our resulting spiritual progress is to be evident to all. Bill is keeping the evidence hidden. But as Bill's mind and life are programmed with these concepts, he should begin to process the data of opportunities to share and take advantage of them — in spite of the fact that he is shy and retiring.

But what if Bill doesn't know anything about his responsibility to share? Is he then out of the will of God? Yes, but in a passive rather than an active sense. Being unaware of God's desire in this matter, Bill is not consciously and deliberately choosing to act against God's will. He is failing to do what God wants him to do, but because he does not know this, his failure is attributed to ignorance rather than to intentional, willful sin. We are responsible to act on what we know. James puts it this way: "Therefore, to one who knows the right thing to do, and does it not, to him it is sin" (4:17). If Bill doesn't know these concepts, he is not accountable for them. But we can't let him go scot free. As a new Christian, he is to have the appetite of a newborn babe for the Word so that he can grow (1 Peter 2:2). If he is not avidly learning truths like the above, then he is out of the will of God. And by the way, if other Christians are failing to teach him such truths, they are out of the will of God! (Col. 3:16; Heb. 10:24).

Try 1 John 3:17. "But whoever has the world's goods, and beholds his brother in need and closes his heart against him, how does the love of God abide in him?" If you see somebody in need and you can meet that person's need but do not, you aren't loving as God expects you to. The data? A leaky faucet. It's been dripping for weeks. Your wife has asked you to fix it and you promised her you would, but you just haven't been able to get to it yet. There are so many other things on your schedule. You have to work, eat, sleep, watch television, play golf, fix the car, etc. But you could fix it. You have the right tools and enough plumbing know-how. If you could just find the time. What is the will of God in the matter? If you are pro-grammed to love your wife by acting to meet her needs, then, because right now she needs to have a dripping faucet repaired, you have only one legitimate response to be in the will of God: Get your tools and head for the sink! The Word of God will program us to love. When the data of human needs confront us, we will respond to meet those needs and in so doing we will demonstrate the love of God.

Now try some situations on your own. Look up each Scripture reference and work through the issue in the light of the Word.

Mary tends to stretch her coffee break beyond the allotted time. Programmed with Colossians 3:23, 24, how would she change?

Paul is going with a non-Christian girl and they are starting to get serious. If he is programmed with 2 Corinthians 6:14-18, what will he do?

The Johnstons are careful not to miss church unless it is absolutely necessary. What passage(s) of Scripture would you say they are programmed with?

Beverly is legitimately upset with some things in her husband's life but she is repressing her feelings of anger and not saying anything. Programmed with Ephesians 4:25, 26, 29, how would she respond?

Pastor Thomas is very hesitant to confront his people on an individual basis with regard to their needs and problems. What would his approach to ministry be if he were programmed with Colossians 1:28?

The members of Grace Church are used to having the pastor do most of the studying and communicating of truth. If they were programmed with Romans 15:14, what changes might take place?

Life is composed largely of decisions and we make our decisions on the basis of the data we have and the way we are programmed. I cannot know and do the will of God apart from the Word of God, but just knowing the Word does not guarantee that I will automatically know and do God's will. I must relate the Word to the situation and the situation to the Word and then, led by the Spirit of God, make the decision. If I have correctly applied the Word of God in that situation, then I will have done the will of God.

Colossians 1:9, 10 shows us how knowing the Word and applying the Word are to be tied together. Paul says in verse 9 that he is praying that these believers will be "filled with the knowledge of His will in all spiritual wisdom and understanding." The "knowledge of His will" is something we are to be saturated with. The only place to get the knowledge of His will is from the Word of God. We are to assimilate Scripture in such a way that we become spiritually wise and understanding. What do we do with this knowledge and wisdom and understanding we have about the will of God? Verse 10 tells us what the purpose of this spiritual insight is:

> . . . so that you may walk in a manner worthy of the Lord, to please Him in all respects, bearing fruit in every good work and increasing in the knowledge of God.

We know the will of God in order to do the will of God. Though we often tend to think of the will of God in reference to major issues and decisions such as what school to attend, which vocation to pursue, whom to marry, where to live, etc., the Scriptures link it to our *total* life. We are to "please Him in *all* respects" and to bear fruit "in *every* good work." No part of life is exempt from the will of God.

Sometimes the will of God is simple and clear. We would hardly pause in making the decision not to falsify our income tax return. We would automatically compliment a friend on a job well done. Many aspects of the will of God come very naturally to us. This is usually because of good teaching and training we have received in our homes and in our churches.

But in other situations we have to struggle to process the data and struggle to make the right decision. Paul recognizes this and comments on it in Ephesians 5. In verse 8 he exhorts his readers to "walk as children of light." In verse 10 he says that such a walk involves the diligent effort of "trying to learn what is pleasing to the Lord." "Trying to learn" is a translation of the same Greek word translated "prove" in Romans 12:2. Walking as children of the light involves the ongoing process of testing to discover what is pleasing to the Lord. "Pleasing" is the same word translated "acceptable" in Romans 12:2; so the apostle is developing essentially the same ideas in these two passages. The same thought is picked up again in verses 15 through 17:

> Therefore be careful how you walk, not as unwise men, but as wise, making the most of your time, because the days are evil. So then do not be foolish, but understand what the will of the Lord is.

Note the last clause: "but understand what the will of the Lord is." The word for "understanding" is not the usual one that Paul uses. This word literally means "to bring together." The Greek world viewed understanding as a process of bringing things together. Paul uses the word here to show that understanding the will of God may not be a flash of instant insight but, rather, a prolonged process of putting the pieces of the puzzle together and finally arriving at the knowledge of God's will in a particular situation. A college student seeking to determine his major field

Processing the data from your world

The computer that is being programmed is ready to process data. The believer who is properly programmed with the Word is ready to process the data from his world in a proper and understanding way.

Romans 12:1, 2 talks about data processing. The key concept in verse 1 is *presentation*. On the basis of what God has done for us in Christ, we are asked to make ourselves available as living sacrifices to God. The *program* is stated negatively: "Do not be conformed to this world" and then positively: "but be transformed." Transformation means change — the kind of change that produces growth toward Christlikeness. It is to be a continual transformation as shown by the present tense of the verb. This comes about as the result of a *process* — "the renewing of your mind." To renew the mind is to be programmed by the Word. There is no life transformation apart from the renewing of the mind. The *purpose* of this presentation, program, and process is "that you may prove what the will of God is." "Prove" is a word similar to *anakrino* used in 1 Corinthians 2:14, 15. It means to test in order to approve, to certify, to accredit. The believer whose mind is being renewed is programmed to process data from his life — to test it in order to discover what the will of God is. You do not discover the will of God simply by amassing a set of biblical facts. These facts must be related to life. Life gives us another set of facts. We process these facts according to the way we are programmed.

For example: Your child disobeys you. You process the "data of disobedience" in terms of the way you are programmed. If you are programmed to think permissively, you may let the child get away with it. If you are programmed to think biblically, you may administer discipline. In either case, you will go through the experience of processing the data in order to "prove" what the will of God is for you and for your child in that given instance. The data you process will be external, i.e., from the child and perhaps from your mate; there will also be internal data from your own thoughts and feelings and background. How you process it and the decision you make will of study may spend many months listening, reading, talking, thinking, and praying — putting it all together to discover God's will in terms of a course of study. A businessman will go through a similar process as he seeks to decide whether to change jobs. Where the Bible does not reveal specific answers (as in the above two illustrations), the believer must go through the process of relating all of the relevant situational data to all of the relevant biblical principles and precepts. Such struggles take time and effort, but they inevitably help us to increase in the knowledge of God (Col. 1:10).

Last week we received in the mail a check for $20.00 made out to me. It was from an insurance company reimbursing us for one of our daughters' visit to the doctor for minor surgery. There was only one problem with it. Our daughter was not covered under this policy; only I was. Apparently the doctor sent the bill to the insurance company where somebody mistakenly approved the claim, and the check was issued. We are programmed with the concept of *honesty*, but we struggled for nearly a week trying to decide what to do with that check. We found ourselves thinking of reasons why we should just go ahead and cash it. It is amazing how one can rationalize when money is involved. I even thought to myself at one point, *It must have been God's will to supply us with additional funds He knew we needed.* It was obviously His determined will to have the check sent to us, but there was no way we could conclude that it was His desired will for us to keep the check. We ultimately processed the data according to the way we were programmed and sent it back.

Let's summarize. My world continually gives me all kinds of data. I receive it and then process it. If I am being programmed by the Word of God, I process it on that basis, and the print-out I get is an indication of the will of God in the matter.

6

The Will of God
and Your World

The significance of your world

So far our thrust has been to make the believer Word-oriented, for without the Word of God he can't really know the will of God. But the Word-oriented believer lives in the world and it is in this world that he does the will of God. The world then becomes the context for the discovery and doing of the will of God. The experiences of life are the fabric on which we weave our decisions to be and do what God wants. The Lord made it clear that Christians are to be *in* the world but not *of* the world, and then while *in* the world they were to be sanctified *in* the truth (John 17:15-19). To be in the truth while in the world is to be *in* the will of God. You do not find the will of God *from* the world, but you do find it *in* the world, that is, the world offers us both the data that help us discover it and the place in which we do it. The Christian's environment is the stage on which he plays out the will of God. It is also the prompter from which he gets some cues and the place where other actors give him input so that he knows what to do. But the script is the Word of God, and that is basic. Sometimes the actors help and support and at other times they do not. But the basic point is that you do not act it out sitting in the audience. You act on the stage.

The theology of your world

The deist says the world is like a clock that God has made and wound up and then left to run on its own. He is a God who doesn't interfere, who is not involved — an absentee God. The pantheist says no. God is everywhere and in everything. He is so much involved in life and so much a part of everything that He really doesn't exist apart from this world. The Bible says that elements of both views are true. God is the creator and sustainer, who exists apart from this world. Yet God is also and at the same time intimately involved in every facet of the world He has created. Isaiah 40 captures both aspects of God as the writer reveals that the one who "sits above the vault of the earth" (v. 22) is the same one who "gives strength to the weary" (v. 29). Paul treats the same two concepts when he says in Acts 17 that "God who made the world and all things in it . . . does not dwell in temples made with hands" (v. 24) is also the God who "is not far from each one of us" (v. 27).

The world in which we live is a world in which God is at work. He is working all things after the counsel of His own will (Eph. 1:11). He is causing all of these things to work together for a good purpose (Rom. 8:28). "He causes His sun to rise on the evil and the good, and sends rain on the righteous and the unrighteous" (Matt. 5:45). He does not leave Himself without a witness, for He does good and gives rains from heaven and fruitful seasons (Acts 14:17). The blessing of food to eat and the capacity to enjoy marriage are gifts from the hand of a gracious God (1 Tim. 4:3, 4). Money and the capacity to buy and enjoy material possessions are furnished to us by God (1 Tim. 6:17). Directly and indirectly God is actively involved in our world and thus in our individual lives. Now we can begin to appreciate how the world can be the context for us to know and do the will of God. We are His people, governed and guided by His Word, seeking to discover and do His will, all in the context of His

48

world. In biblical hermeneutics, the *context* is important for the proper interpretation of the particular *text*. In practical hermeneutics the same is true. The believer seeks to interpret the Word of God (the text) in the world of God (the context), in order to find the will of God (the meaning, the interpretation). The context is not primary but it is important in discovering God's will.

An illustration

In the city hall a statute has been placed on the books: There is a 15 MPH speed limit in school zones during school hours. This is a precept — a law. It is based on the principle that we should guard the lives and safety of smaller children when they are crossing streets going to and from school. This precept is revealed to the general public by placing signs at school crossings, informing motorists of the specific details of the precept: "SCHOOL ZONE, 15 MPH DURING SCHOOL HOURS." It's the desired will of the city.

Of course, the sign does not exist in a vacuum. There are many other factors in the context that call our attention to the sign and its message. These are such things as the school building and the children playing in the schoolyard. There are usually different colored lines marking the crosswalk. There may be uniformed children with flags acting as crosswalk guards. There could be a policeman or a patrol car in the area. Your car has a speedometer that tells you how fast you are going and brakes to help you slow down. There are often other cars going through the school zone at the same time; some too fast and others at the right speed. You may even have a back-seat driver furnishing you with completely unsolicited information on how to handle the situation! The school zone may stir up memories of an accident that occurred in the past to you or someone you know. Then there is your conscience that whispers, "Slow down." Furthermore, God has provided you with eyes to see all of these things, ears to hear those sounds that are significant, a mind to interpret all of the relevant data, and a will to make a decision. The sign is surrounded by all of these factors. They are present to enable us to understand the sign and to prompt us to obey it. They help us to know and do the will of the city officials — slow down to 15 MPH.

In a similar fashion, God has revealed in His Word through precept and principle what He wants us to be and to do. He has made it clear to us, and our responsibility is to know it and do it. At the same time, we live in His world and He has furnished us with numerous other factors that He uses to call our attention to the precepts and principles in His Word. He also uses these same factors as a providentially arranged context to help us understand His will and encourage us to do it.

The other factors

a. *external:*

circumstances	— God uses the incidents of our lives to help us find His will.
counsel	— Individuals will cross our paths and give us words of wisdom and insight that will aid us in walking worthy of our calling.
consequences	— Both the pleasant and the unpleasant results of our actions alert us to what God's will is or was.

b. *internal:*

common sense	— Our ability to think intelligently and logically can be utilized to help us discover the will of God.
compulsion	— Those inner inclinations to do or not do can be guidelines to God's will.
conscience	— Our internal moral monitor will be brought to play as we determine what God wants to happen in our lives.
contentment	— How we feel about some action is also an important factor in deciding if it is God's will for us.

In the next few chapters we will investigate each of these to determine both biblically and practically how God can and does work in His world to help us discover and do His will.

7

Circumstances and the Will of God

Circumstantial evidence ought to be highly important to the Christian. Things don't "just happen" to one who firmly believes in a God who is in control of the world in general and his life in particular. Whether it is a stub of the toe, the loss of a job, the chance meeting of an old friend, the ring of a phone, or the unexpected check in the mail — the believer must learn to consider the circumstances. Why? Because God can and does use circumstances to help us discover and do His will.

God is involved

God is involved in all the circumstances of our lives. Ephesians 1:11 states that He "works all things after the counsel of His will." The context deals with the fact that salvation in all of its grandeur is ours because of what God has done for us in Christ. What has happened to the believer has happened because God is at work. As a matter of fact, says Paul, He is working all things (salvation and everything else) according to the counsel of his will. *Counsel* involves the idea of deliberation and decision. *Will* involves the desire. The divine mind is not in a state of indifference. God has an inclination to do something and He does it.

He doesn't consult with anyone else. What He wants to do, He decides to do. God is in charge of all things from beginning to end. This includes all of the incidents of your life and mine. The three key words in this verse are "working" (emphasizing the activity of God), "counsel" (emphasizing the wisdom of God), and "will" (emphasizing the sovereignty of God). God is actively at work in all things, and He does what He wants to do. Place this truth alongside every incident in your life: He works all things according to the counsel of His will.

Romans 8:28 further elaborates on the concept of God at work in our lives:

> And we know that God causes all things to work together for good to those who love God, to those who are called according to His purpose.

Notice that all things "work together." The events of our lives do not happen at random; they are synchronized by God for a good purpose. Events are not isolated in God's plan; they are integrated. They all have a purpose, which is described in one word — "good." Here the "all things" refers to even the sufferings of life (v. 18). "Work together" means that each element plays its appointed part in our lives — put in its place by God. The individual events may in themselves not be classified as good, but in the end a good purpose is achieved. This kind of circumstantial insight is present most concretely in the minds of those who "love God." Loving God is our subjective response, which then makes us aware of God at work in our lives. The objective reason is given at the end of the verse — we are "called according to His purpose." We are called into a relationship with Him that involves His purpose for us. Thus both a divine side and a human side are presented. Our attitude and His action combine to make us keenly aware of the reality of the sovereignty of God in every area of our lives.

Let us go one step farther. God is not only involved in everything that happens in our lives and in programming it all for a good purpose, but He uses every conceivable type of incident to accomplish this good purpose. Ecclesiastes 7:13, 14 is a profound presentation of this fact.

> Consider the work of God,
> For who is able to straighten what He has bent?
> In the day of prosperity be happy,
> But in the day of adversity consider —
> God has made the one as well as the other
> So that man may not discover anything that will be after him.

In verses 11 and 12 the writer, Solomon, comments on the value of wisdom — it adds a dimension to life. For example, the person with real wisdom knows how God works, and in verses 13 and 14 he shares insight on this issue. Solomon reminds them of the reality of the sovereignty of God by referring to the "work of God." "Work" ought to ring a familiar note, since we just saw it in both Ephesians 1:11 and Romans 8:28. Our response to the fact that God is at work is to consider it, to think about it. Paul appeals to the intellect in Romans 8:28 when he says, "We *know* that God causes all things to work together. . . ." Doctrine needs to be implanted in the mind. Thinking is basic to living. In the last half of verse 13 the author shows the relationship of the sovereign God to human life. He asks, "Who is able to straighten what He has bent?" The question is designed to demonstrate three things. First, it shows what life is really like for each of us. It is bent, crooked! It has its ups and downs. It has thrills and it has tragedies. Second, it demonstrates what God can do. He bends life for us. He is involved in the ups and downs, the rough and the smooth. Third, it shows what man cannot do. Man cannot straighten what God has bent! When God puts a curve in man's road, man cannot straighten it out. When the air goes *whoosh* out of that rear tire when, in God's providence, we have just run over a nail, we can't back up and reverse the circumstances so that the nail is removed and the air is replaced. What a unique way to show that God is sovereignly involved. He "bends" the circumstances of our lives.

"Who is able to straighten what He has bent?" The answer

is obvious. No one. Verse 14 gives us a set of instructions telling us how to react to the circumstances of life that God has allowed to be present. "In the day of prosperity be happy." When things are going well, when the way is straight — rejoice. As a rule, we don't have to be told to do that. When things are going great, we know it and we feel good. But then comes "the day of adversity." That's when things don't go so well. The sinus headache hits. The car breaks down. The bus is late. The check doesn't arrive. The baby cries all night. How do we respond? Our temptation is to get frustrated and depressed, but our instructions are to *think!* We are to *consider* carefully the fact that God is at work, that He has made the one (the day of prosperity) as well as the other (the day of adversity). He programs both the prosperity and the adversity into our lives. Sometimes they come one right next to the other — without any advance notice.

I was at Arcadia High School in Phoenix, Arizona, watching my son Jim throw the discus in a track meet. He was throwing well and when the competition was over and the measurements were made, he came running over to me with the news that he had not only won but had broken the school record. As a freshman he had thrown the discus farther than any freshman before him. For his father this was a moment of prosperity! I was happy! All that talent packed into one boy! He undoubtedly had inherited it from his father! I was leaning against the fence indulging in this moment of immense prosperity when my wife and three other children arrived. I informed them of Jim's achievements and they rejoiced with me. But then my wife, Audrey, brought her news into the arena. "Dr. Mattson just called about the pathology report on the mole you had removed this week. You've got cancer." I went from prosperity to adversity. At that point and for the next few days I had to struggle personally with the fact that God was at work in my own life. I had to reflect thoughtfully on the fact that God had allowed this set of circumstances to invade my experience. I had to learn to accept it — and it wasn't easy. Three days later I had extensive surgery and to this date there has been no recurrence of the malignancy.

56

Why does God operate this way in our lives? Why does He program prosperity and adversity into our experience, often moving from one to the other without warning? The reason is simply stated in verse 14: "so that man may not discover anything that will be after him." When God does it this way, we don't know with absolute certainty what's coming next. This is not to keep us guessing but trusting. Proverbs 3:6 is pertinent: "in all your ways acknowledge Him." If life for us were nothing but smooth, straight roads, we would grow so self-confident that we would soon say to the Lord, "Leave the driving to us!" Those who build freeways plan gentle curves and hills and valleys to keep drivers alert. When the roads are completely straight and smooth, drivers are mesmerized by the changeless ribbons of concrete — they tend to grow careless or fall asleep. Christians would do the same if life were perpetually placid. God programs curves, ruts, and even detours to keep us alert and trusting.

So we have seen that God is involved in the circumstances of our lives. We need to remind ourselves of this constantly and realize that this involvement is to help us know and do His will. For example, in Acts 1:8 the Lord Jesus outlined His will for the disciples. They were to be witnesses at home in Jerusalem and then in Judea and Samaria and eventually to every part of the world. In Acts 8:1 we see God at work through the circumstances of persecution, driving the disciples out of Jerusalem into Judea and Samaria. His will was their witness beyond Jerusalem. The pressure of persecution caused them to move. According to Philippians 1:12-14, Paul views the circumstances of his imprisonment as causing the progress of the gospel. He comments on the beneficial effects of a strong letter he had written to the Corinthian Christians, indicating that it had caused them to sorrow to the point of repentance (2 Cor. 7:8-10).

Christians ought to be sensitive to circumstances. Health; job transfers; financial situations; and international, national, local, family, and personal situations ought to be read in terms of what God wants us to know and do. When we read of a highway

57

tragedy, we ought to become more careful ourselves as we drive. If I am overweight and out of breath, I need to evaluate my diet and exercise program.

One summer my wife and I flew to Israel for a two-week visit. We arrived on a Friday at Tel Aviv airport. Our luggage didn't. For five days and nights we had to manage with the clothes we were wearing and the toothpaste and toothbrushes my wife had put in her purse! Unpleasant circumstances, to say the least. But we knew God was involved, so we asked why. And the answers came to us from the Word. John 15:5 said, "Apart from Me you can do nothing." Until then our approach had been "As long as we have our luggage we can do anything!" We were learning to trust more in the Savior and less in our suitcases. Colossians 3:2 also was being impressed on us: "Set your mind on the things above, not on the things that are on earth." The Lord knew that as long as we had our luggage we would tend to be content with things on the earth. So He arranged for a baggage agent in Amsterdam to set our earthly possessions aside for five days.

We don't always have insight in the midst of circumstances. Sometimes we look back with the perspective that God wants us to have. The psalmist did this in Psalm 119:67 with this insightful comment: "Before I was afflicted I went astray, but now I keep Thy Word." He now realized that God applied pressure in order to produce obedience. Hebrews 12:11 tells us that divine discipline in the life of the believer does not seem joyful at the time but that afterwards it yields the peaceful fruit of righteousness. We can look back on many incidents of our lives and see how God was at work in a variety of circumstances. Much of this we could not see when these incidents happened, but as we grow and mature, we should be able to read the circumstances more quickly and accurately. This is the development of the capacity to discern the will of God as stated in Romans 12:2 and elaborated on in Hebrews 5:14, where it is stated that the mature are those who have their senses trained to discern good and evil.

A word of caution

Always check the circumstances with the Word of God. Scripture gives us the authoritative guide to evaluate the circumstantial evidence. We can misread or misinterpret the circumstances. For example, the road is straight; it's late at night; there is no traffic; and there are no patrol cars. Circumstantial evidence might lead us to conclude that it's all right to exceed the speed limit. But the Word says we are to submit ourselves for the Lord's sake to every human institution (1 Peter 2:13) regardless of the circumstances. Even though "the law" isn't there, God is.

He is a good-looking fellow, has a good job and a great personality, and you and he get along on your dates, but he is not a Christian and you are. The circumstances for marriage may read positive, but the Word reads negative (2 Cor. 6:14-18).

Life is loaded with an amazing variety of circumstances for each of us. God is at work in all of them, and we need to be sensitive to His purposes in them. We should learn to interpret the circumstantial evidence and consistently to submit it to the Word. Any insights we get and steps we take that are based on the incidents of our lives must always be in harmony with the clear teaching of Scripture.

8

Counsel and the Will of God

You're facing a tough decision. You aren't sure which choice to make. You want to do God's will but you aren't sure what it is, so you share your dilemma with a trusted friend. You receive some additional input from your friend and then you make your decision. Is this the right route for a believer? Should we look to friends for advice and counsel? Can others help us discover and do the will of God?

The case for counsel

It is practical to talk to someone else about the issues we face in our own lives. Just to articulate them helps us understand our own attitudes and ideas on an issue. Listening can also help us gain additional information and insight from the wisdom and experience of others.

It is not only practical, it is also biblical. Believers are related to each other in the body of Christ for ministries to each other. Ephesians 4:15 indicates that growth will take place as members of the body of Christ speak the truth in love. When we ask for advice, we allow this process for growth to take place. In 1 Corinthians 12:25, 26 Paul uses the analogy of the human body to show what ought to be happening in the spiritual body.

> . . . that there should be no division in the body, but that the members should have the same care for one another. And if one member suffers, all the members suffer with it; if one member is honored, all the members rejoice with it.

These verses tell us that Christians are to have a care and concern for each other and that a communications network needs to be active and so personalized that when individual members are suffering or rejoicing, the rest of the body is aware of it. When we are hurting, we are often in need of mature advice and counsel in order to ascertain God's will in the matter. Don't be afraid to ask for counsel and don't be reticent to give it, when asked. Galatians 6:2 is another passage that supports the concept of helping one another. We are exhorted to "bear one another's burdens, and thus fulfil the law of Christ." Sometimes the burden we carry is obvious and those who are spiritually mature should spontaneously reach out to help us. This is the thrust of verse 1 where it is said that one caught in a trespass is to be restored by his mature friends. At other times we can mask our burden so well that others won't know. They cannot help unless we share it with them. We often bear alone what we ought to share.

Scripture is filled with examples of counsel. Jethro gave Moses counsel on administrative procedures (Exod. 18:13-27). Older women are told to counsel younger women (Titus 2:3-5). Believers are instructed to teach and admonish each other (Col. 3:16). Paul speaks of the mutual encouragement that he expects to take place when he and the Christians at Rome get together (Rom. 1:12). As a matter of fact, many of Paul's letters were filled with doctrinal and practical advice to other Christians. Sometimes the advice and counsel were solicited. At other times they were not.

Some people feel it is a sign of weakness to ask for advice and counsel. They have the concept that a mature person will be self-sufficient to handle his or her own problems or perhaps will not even have any problems! Such an attitude violates the biblical concept of the mutual interdependency of the members of the body of Christ. If people who need help do not ask for it, they may never get it, and the whole body will suffer. It is not a sign of weakness to ask for advice and counsel. It is a mark of personal maturity. To know you have a problem, to know you have not been able to solve it yourself, and to know that another member of the body has wisdom and insight you need are all marks of mature thinking. The small child often refuses to let the parent help him with a task that is more than he can handle. Why? Because he doesn't realize that he cannot do the job. That is a mark of immaturity — failure to realize his inability to do it alone. As the child grows, he realizes what he cannot do and learns to ask for help. That is a sign of growth and maturation — not a sign of weakness.

Getting counsel

Although we develop the capacity to handle many issues ourselves, sometimes we will face a problem or decision that looms larger than the normal ones and we need help. Decisions regarding what school I should attend, what course I should take, what career I should pursue, what person I should marry, what job I should take, where I should live, etc., involve some of the prime issues of life and we want to know and do God's will in them. Others can help us find God's will. These are what we might call "fourth-and-one" situations. In a football game when it's "fourth and one," the situation can be very critical if you are in the final two minutes of the game, on your opponents' 25-yard line, and the score is tied. Do you try a field goal or go for a first down? If the latter, what play do you run? A smart, mature quarterback calls time out and goes to the sideline and seeks the counsel of the wisest, most mature, and most experienced man on the sidelines — the coach. The coach not only has the maturity that comes from experience, he also has the maturity that comes from looking at the game from a different perspective; i.e., not only from the sidelines but also from the

63

spotter's vantage point high up in the press box. The quarter-back still has to run the play himself but now he does it with added information and insight.

God puts a lot of coaches along the sidelines for us during our life here on earth. The believer ought to recognize when the fourth-and-one situations are present and take time out, go to the sidelines, and talk to a coach. It may be your mom, dad, pastor, youth minister, teacher, sponsor, or just a close friend whom you respect. But be careful — go to the right sidelines! Get your counsel and advice from those on *your* team. And when you get to your sidelines, go to the coach, not to the water boy or the fourth string tackle who has played only seven minutes all season. As for time-outs — they are unlimited. Call one whenever you need one. One other point: Go while the game is still in progress. For example, a man who knows things are not going well in his marriage but is convinced he can handle it by himself may discover that when he finally goes to the sidelines for help, the game is over and it is too late. Time has run out.

Giving counsel

A word of counsel is now appropriate to those who give counsel. The privilege of helping people discover and do the will of God is an awesome responsibility. Yet one cannot wait until he has arrived at perfection to begin helping others, for then he will never get started! The Scriptures indicate that *all* believers can and should teach and admonish each other (Rom. 15:14; Col. 3:16). The church ought to be a mutual edification society in which *every* member is alert to opportunities to communicate insight. "Teach and admonish" are favorite words of the apostle Paul to describe the nature of our communication. This means our advice should be *instructive*. When we give Word-oriented counsel, it will be instructive. When we give experience-centered counsel, it may be nothing more than opinion. Our personal attitudes, opinions, and biases always need to be related to the Word before we prescribe them as the right medicine for others. Those who teach the Word should recognize that they are communicating counsel regarding the will of God. Pastors, Sunday school teachers, and parents are significantly and consistently involved in doing this. Recognize your strategic position and teach effectively! Furthermore, any believer who in any way communicates to another believer has the potential opportunity to teach him concerning the will of God. When we talk, we teach. So we should make sure we say what God wants us to say and that we say it in a way that the other person can understand it. Every conversation, no matter how casual, is an opportunity to educate all who hear (and this includes the speaker) about the will of God.

Our counsel should also be *corrective*. "Admonish" means "to confront in order to correct." Counsel is never given to someone who is totally neutral. The person brings to the situation such things as bad attitudes, wrong information, failure to act, deliberate misdeeds, etc. Thus, to give adequate counsel concerning the will of God we not only instruct but also confront and correct. "Speaking the truth in love" (Eph. 4:15), we are to present those words that are "good for edification according to the need of the moment" (v. 29). A careful reading of Paul's letters (especially 1 and 2 Corinthians) will furnish one with a pattern for this edifying process of teaching and admonishing. In these letters Paul is giving God-oriented advice — some of it solicited by the Corinthian Christians in previous letters, some of it unsolicited. He told them what they wanted to know. That's instruction. He told them what they needed to know. That's admonition.

Any believer who is growing and maturing is equipped to offer significant counsel to others. Having the capacity both to evaluate the situation and to apply the Word, he can be most helpful to the one who is having trouble understanding the situation and has an inadequate grasp of the truth. Galatians 6:1 refers to such an experience:

> Brethren, even if a man is caught in any trespass, you who are spiritual, restore such a one in a spirit of gentleness; looking to yourself, lest you too be tempted.

The one "caught in any trespass" is out of the will of God. Who provides help? Those who are spiritual. Those who know the Word and have applied it in their own experience (Rom. 12:2). Those who are trained to discern good and evil (Heb. 5:14). Those who can think like Christ (1 Cor. 2:16). Those who have taken the log out of their own eye and are thus able to see clearly enough to take the speck out of their brother's eye (Matt. 7:1-5). They can offer the kind of counsel that "restores" or "equips" a brother or sister in the Lord to function in the will of God. And because theirs is a maturity hammered out on the anvil of their own life, they will offer it with a gentle and meek spirit, knowing full well their own propensity to fail to do God's will. Counsel should never come across as pat answers from a proud heart, but instead, as Word-oriented insights communicated with confident humility from a person who himself is in the process of determining the will of God.

The limitations of counsel

No human being has all the answers. Regardless of how mature your friend is, he doesn't have infinite insight. He is biased, prejudiced, subjective, not fully informed. Be careful of the innate tendency to idolize the counselor. The more we do this, the less we evaluate the counsel we receive. Always evaluate advice and counsel in the light of the Word. Instead of merely asking friends for advice, ask them what they feel the Word of God has to say about your decision or problem. God's will is wrapped up in God's Word. You should seek counsel to find out what the Word says, not just what a friend thinks.

Realize also that though others provide data for us, the responsibility for decision and action is ours. Don't expect or allow others to make decisions for you. If they do, you become weak and dependent rather than strong and independent. You are trying to discover the will of God for your own life. This may involve asking others for counsel, but you must process the data, relate it to the Word of God, and make a responsible decision on your own.

9

Conscience and the Will of God

"Let your conscience be your guide." "He's got a guilty conscience." "My conscience is clear." With these and many other statements we often refer to the conscience — the thinking man's moral filter, as some have called it. What is the conscience? Can it be involved in knowing and doing the will of God?

The nature of the conscience

The Word of God tells us that the human conscience is a reality and that it is our innate and intuitive capacity to distinguish between right and wrong. A primary passage is Romans 2:14, 15:

> For when Gentiles who do not have the Law do instinctively the things of the Law, these, not having the Law, are a law to themselves, in that they show the work of the Law written in their hearts, their conscience bearing witness, and their thoughts alternately accusing or else defending themselves.

This passage teaches us that God's moral law is written internally into the fiber of every human being and that we all instinctively respond to it. There is no such thing as a person or a society without moral values. God has programmed moral values into each human being. The passage goes on to teach that each person has a conscience that bears witness to the reality of this inner moral law. The conscience is an active, operative function in the human being. Finally, we see that the person with an active conscience is mentally aware of whether his attitudes and actions are right or wrong. In his mind he is passing judgment on himself — determining whether he is guilty and thus to be accused, or innocent and thus able to defend his conduct. This passage makes a clear distinction between the mind and the conscience. They are viewed as two different functions. The same distinction is seen in Titus 1:15 where it is indicated that "both their mind and their conscience are defiled." It is man's moral intuition that witnesses to his mind. The moral intuition does not have *volition* but it does have *values*. It makes value judgments on our attitudes and actions — those contemplated and those completed. It is our sensitivity to our moral responsibility and it functions to approve the good and to condemn the bad. Paul refers to this in his own life in two instances. In Romans 9:1 he says, "I am telling the truth in Christ, I am not lying, my conscience bearing me witness in the Holy Spirit." His conscience is supporting to his own satisfaction the fact that he is telling the truth. In 2 Corinthians 1:12 he tells his readers that his conscience is giving him positive feedback regarding the fact that he has conducted himself in the world in general and toward them in particular "in holiness and godly sincerity."

The conscience may be compared to the human sense of taste. Our taste buds monitor the food we put into our mouth and transmit this information to our minds. If the food is sweet, the taste buds witness to this fact. If the food is sour, the taste buds communicate that information. If the food is rancid, the taste buds let us know that, too. Because we have taste buds, we can evaluate and pass judgment on all the food that enters our mouths.

A good, clear conscience

At this point we can see that the person who is living in the will of God will be getting positive feedback from his conscience, whereas the person out of the will of God will be getting negative feedback from his conscience. Thus the stress in the New Testament is for the believer to have a *good* conscience, a *clear* conscience, and a *blameless* conscience before men and God. Note the following verses:

> And Paul, looking intently at the Council, said, "Brethren, I have lived my life with a perfectly *good conscience* before God up to this day" (Acts 23:1).
>
> In view of this, I also do my best to maintain always a *blameless conscience* both before God and before men (Acts 24:16).
>
> The goal of our instruction is love from a pure heart and a *good conscience* and a sincere faith (1 Tim. 1:5).
>
> Deacons . . . holding to the mystery of the faith with a *clear conscience* (1 Tim. 3:8, 9).
>
> I thank God, whom I serve with a *clear conscience* . . . (2 Tim. 1:3).

Hebrews makes it clear that the Christian is one who has accepted Christ as his Savior and as a result has his conscience cleansed from the guilt and penalty of his sins (cf. Heb. 9:9, 14; 10:2, 22). This burden has been lifted from the conscience of the believer. But his conscience still functions to monitor his thoughts and actions. The ideal is for the believer to be obedient to the Word of God and thus his conscience will be giving him positive feedback. Positive feedback is important. David got negative feedback for a prolonged period of time while living in unconfessed sin, and he was miserable (Psalm 32:3, 4). When he confessed, he obtained relief (vv. 1, 2, 5). To live with a conscience giving us negative data is to be emotionally and mentally miserable. That's the price we pay for being out of the will of God.

If we are thinking of doing something wrong, our conscience may warn us, "That's wrong; don't do it." If we go ahead and do it, the conscience convicts us by saying, "You did it; you shouldn't have done it." The conscience doesn't prevent us from doing the wrong thing but it can keep us from enjoying having done it! When considering the right course of action, the conscience will approve, and after we have done the right thing, the conscience will continue to approve and validate the decision. Thus, the conscience can very definitely be an aid to knowing and doing God's will.

The malfunction of the conscience

The Christian can have a *weak* conscience. This is caused by *inadequate or improper knowledge.* This point is made clear in 1 Corinthians 8. Some believers were having problems with the eating of meat that had been sacrificed to idols. Their knowledge was improper in that they felt such meat was in some way spiritually polluted for them. Their knowledge was inadequate in that they did not realize the idol had no capacity to change anything; only God has that capacity (8:1-6). Without this knowledge their conscience was classified as *weak*, and when they ate meat that had been sacrificed to idols, their conscience gave them negative feedback and they felt guilty (8:7). But that kind of guilt is not necessary. Adequate knowledge of the Word of God will furnish the conscience with proper facts and enable it to be accurately sensitive.

Many Christians have weak consciences in various areas and thus are confused about what the will of God is. But when the mind is renewed with the Word of God, the conscience can function properly. When it is not fed biblical data, it may become either too strict or too lenient. In other words, the human conscience is fallible and flexible. When it is influenced by inadequate and/or inaccurate input, it will begin to function improperly. According to 1 Corinthians 8, it is clear that the believer who has the stronger (more knowledgeable) conscience is, in love, to be careful to do only that which edifies the weak believer. There could be a time then when the strong believer would not eat meat sacrificed to idols in order not to offend the weak believer (8:8-13). However, that approach is not the only thing to be done. The other is to teach the weak believer so he can function more maturely. The strong are to be sensitive to the needs of the weak.

The untaught, ignorant believer will have trouble with the will of God. If his background was quite permissive, he will have a conscience that allows him to do many things that are actually not in accord with the will of God. If it was quite restrictive, he will have a conscience that prohibits him from doing many things that do not violate God's will. When he violates this conscience, he defiles it; that is, he feels a consciousness of guilt. But if he is weak, his conscience is not functioning properly, and he has unnecessary guilt. This is psychological guilt, which means feelings of guilt. In this case his guilt feelings are based on the wrong facts. To feel guilty when one is not actually guilty is to miss God's best for our lives.

On the other hand, it is possible for us to violate our conscience when it has given us the proper facts. This produces real, moral guilt and should be handled with repentance and confession (cf. 1 John 1:9; 2 Cor. 7:9, 10). When the conscience is giving us the right input and we continually reject it, the conscience becomes *seared*, that is, calloused and insensitive. Those who function in this way are fair prey for deceitful spirits and the doctrines of demons (1 Tim. 4:1, 2).

Summary

Every believer has a conscience. It is sensitive to what is right and what is wrong. As the believer grows in the grace and knowledge of the Lord, he becomes more and more aware of what is right and what is wrong — what the will of God is for his life. Thus, his conscience becomes more sensitive and more functional in helping the believer discover the will of God.

Though we have treated the conscience as distinct from the other factors in our personality, we actually function as integrated persons — persons who are both complex and holistic. This means that our conscience is tied to our intellect, feelings, and will. It is the moral dimension in all of these. If I don't "feel" right about a course of action, the conscience is at work. If I "think" that something is wrong for me, my conscience has issued its insight.

All of this points out the significance of the home. Parents are God's appointed teachers (Eph. 6:4). We are put in a position where for fifteen to twenty years we teach our children what is right and what is wrong. We educate their consciences. We do this because we want them to grow up to be mature, law-abiding citizens, functioning properly in every area of life. We want them to grow up to know and do the will of God. Those who have been raised in a strict, legalistic environment may grow up with a super sensitive, overly strict conscience. Parents need to teach their children the truth instead of communicating prejudice and bias and man-made traditions. To communicate to children distorted values, such as that sex is dirty, fun is wrong, and acceptance is based on obedience, is to make it difficult for them to discover and do the will of God. Discipline is a key factor in the overall development of the conscience. Consistently and lovingly applied, it can be a powerful factor in the education and training of the conscience.

The local church should assume its God-given responsibility of equipping adults to function in their world as mature persons, partners, and parents. Such a program will provide their consciences with basic biblical data so they can discover and do the will of God and teach their children to do the same.

10

Common Sense and the
Will of God

The case for common sense

A very practical case can be made for common sense. It is
built on two premises: (1) people are thinking beings; (2) they
live in a predictable world. You know that if you don't get
enough sleep, you get tired. If you play with fire, you get
burned. If you disobey the rules, you get into trouble. If you do
an act of kindness, you feel good. If you repeat an action over
and over, it becomes a habit. All of the above consequences are
predictable and, because we are thinking people, we can predict
that these things will happen. Thus, thinking people living in
such a predictable environment develop and use something we
call common sense. Those who do not have it and/or use it
cannot or do not think and/or cannot or do not know their
environment. For example, a small child does not have much
common sense because he has not had much exposure to life as
yet. An older child should have more common sense and an
adult should have still more.

Common sense is not only practical, it is also scriptural.
Even common sense would cause us to assume it to be so. Who

73

made our minds? Who gave us the capacity to think and reason and reflect? God did. Who made the world with its predictability? God did. Then who is the ultimate author of common sense? *God is!* We would expect the Word of God to refer to it and even to tell us to use it. It does.

The concept of a "sober" or "sound" mind underscores the reality of common sense in the Bible. Notice the interesting exchange of words that Paul had with King Festus Agrippa:

> And while Paul was saying this in his defense, Festus said in a loud voice, "Paul, you are out of your mind! Your great learning is driving you mad." But Paul said, "I am not out of my mind, most excellent Festus, but I utter words of sober truth" (Acts 26:24, 25).

The king told Paul he was presenting an irrational gospel. Paul said he was not doing any such thing, but was communicating words of "sober truth." "Sober" is a translation of the Greek word *sōphrosynē*, which means "soundness of mind," "good sense," or "sanity." "The gospel is both true and rational," says Paul. Even though it may not appeal to natural human reason (1 Cor. 2:14), yet the basic elements of the gospel are reasonable and logical. Our presentation of the gospel should be one that makes sense. The unbeliever may not accept it, but he ought to understand it.

In Romans 12:3 the Christian is instructed not to think more highly of himself than he ought to think, but to think so as to have sound judgment. The infinitive form of the same Greek word is used. The Word is telling us that we are to think sanely and sensibly about ourselves. Knowing that we are saved and gifted for service enables us to have a proper concept of ourselves. If my thoughts about myself are too high or too low, I am not making good sense, and when I am not making good sense about who I am, I am not in God's will.

Peter exhorts believers in 1 Peter 4:7 to live *sensibly* and soberly in the light of the imminent coming of Christ. One of the qualifications for the overseer in 1 Timothy 3:2 is this quality of common sense (prudence, NASB). In 2 Timothy 1:7 the Holy

Spirit's ministry in the life of Timothy is said to have three characteristics — power, love, and discipline (sound judgment, NASB margin). Paul's instructions to Titus are replete with references to common sense. Older men are to be "sensible" (Titus 2:2); older women are to train younger women to be "sensible" (v. 5); and the instructions concerning the younger men are limited to one thing: They should "be sensible" (v. 6).

Then in Titus 2:11, 12 the grace of God is said to be involved in training each believer to deny ungodliness and worldly desires and to live *sensibly*, righteously, and godly in the present age. The grace of God, the Spirit of God, the gospel of God, and godly leaders are all intended to help us to be characterized by sensible soundmindedness. Common sense is biblical. The Spirit-controlled believer ought to be one who uses his head.

The use of common sense

Consider your physical health. Your body is the temple of the Holy Spirit. The Word reveals this in 1 Corinthians 6:19. But the Bible is not a textbook on physical fitness and the prevention and cure of disease. Medical science has discovered much truth about the human body and how to care for it. This is common sense for the Christian and it ought to be put to use. The Bible does not tell us how much sleep we should have but it does tell us to live sensibly. It makes sense to get from six to eight hours of sleep every night. To operate on four or five hours of sleep is to violate sensible care of the body and to be out of the will of God. To overeat is to build up body weight, which puts a strain on the heart, and this doesn't make sense. To overeat and be overweight is to be out of the will of God. To fail to get exercise that keeps the body in tone and the heart in shape is to live stupidly, it is not using one's God-given ability to think things through. To put it more bluntly, the person who isn't getting consistent exercise is out of the will of God, unless of course there are physical reasons why he cannot do so. It makes sense to have a yearly physical examination. It does not make sense to push oneself to the point of physical and emotional exhaustion every day. It is wise to plan times of rest and relaxation every day, every week, and every year. It is foolish to use alcohol, drugs, and tobacco when one knows there is a possibility of addiction or disease occurring.

The Bible says much about money, but it is not a complete textbook on financial affairs. Even so, we are not left groping for guidance: we have our God-given ability to *think*! If we consistently apply common sense to our attitude toward and use of money, we will avoid many problems. It makes sense not to spend more than you make. Those who knowingly and consistently incur expenses greater than their income are out of the will of God. It makes sense to save money for emergencies. Those who do not are out of the will of God. It makes sense to buy quality products that will last much longer and give better service than to buy cheap merchandise and replace it two or three times in the same period. To put it more bluntly, the Christian who spends much of his time shopping for bargains could be out of the will of God. Some years ago a perceptive Christian furniture saleswoman said to me, "All of my Christian customers want to go the cheap route. I try to convince them that furniture is an investment and they ought to buy quality now — pay more for it — and use it and enjoy it for many more years." A well-known Christian leader told me he can no longer justify driving to speaking engagements. Even though it may be cheaper, it takes much longer and he arrives tired. In other words, it makes sense to fly, and because it makes sense, he feels it is God's will.

Are you a student? The Bible does not tell you how and when to study, but it does tell you to use your head. When you do, you read the daily assignments *daily*! You do research for the term paper days or weeks before you write it, not the night before. You ask questions in class so that you get to know your professors, and let them know when you do not understand. These procedures make sense. If you are not consistently functioning in this way, you are out of the will of God.

Common sense is very important in marriage and family relationships. To bring up a touchy issue when your wife is tired is not using your head. It could be the right thing at the wrong time and thus be out of the will of God. To tell your children they *never* do anything right is to make a statement that does not make sense. Once in a while they do something right!

The Word does speak out on many issues in either precept or principles, but in many areas it does not tell us what to do or not to do. How do we proceed and remain in the will of God? One basic suggestion: use your head. Do what makes sense. As a rule, that will put you squarely in the middle of the will of God.

The limitations of common sense

Common sense is not *complete* sense. We do not always have all the facts and we do not always know all the answers. We are finite beings with mental limitations. Though we strive to get as many facts as we can, we consistently fall short of omniscience. Thus we need to check our common sense with the Word of God.

Common sense is not *perfect* sense. The human mind tends to stray and deviate (Jer. 17:9). We can sometimes convince ourselves that black is white and vice versa. The only legitimate corrective and guide is the Word of God. It provides the standard to evaluate and assist our common sense.

God's will may be contrary to what seems to make sense to us. Blessed as we are with the capacity to reason, we remain fallen and finite in intellect. God's thoughts are higher than our thoughts and His ways are higher than our ways (Isa. 55:8, 9). As a rule, the Lord leads Christians to do that which is sensible by our standards, but there are exceptions.

My brother-in-law spent his first years as a missionary in Borneo, working in an area so remote that it took thirty days to go in by boat and on foot. He and his wife made this trip many times in order to minister to a small tribe of Dyack headhunters whose response to the gospel was painfully slow. To many of his friends it did not make sense, but to him it was God's will.

77

I counseled with a young Stanford University student who said he thought he would go on to law school and get a good job, then in his spare time he would work with Young Life and with his good salary totally support two full-time Young Life workers. I said, "That makes sense to me." It did to him too, but gradually he felt compelled to forget all of that, go to seminary himself, and enter the ministry.

God is not bound by our definition of common sense. He delights in doing the different as well as the typical. Thus the believer needs to be constantly checking his intellectual processes with the Word. God will never lead contrary to His Word but He may lead contrary to what we regard as a sensible course of action. The believer needs to be aware of the significance of human reason in discovering the will of God, but he must also be aware that the reason that is significant may not always be sufficient. The Word of God is sufficient on those issues to which it addresses itself. Proverbs 3:5 tells us not to lean on our own understanding. This does not mean we are not to use our own minds, but that we are not to rely solely on them.

11

Compulsion and the Will of God

Not only the mind but also the will is involved in discovering and doing the will of God. Let us look at the way we live and then relate it to the way God works.

The way we live

As we grow and mature and study, we eliminate many possible vocations we might follow, and gravitate toward certain specific ones. We become interested in a particular career. We begin to experience an inner desire to study in that field, major in it, work in it, become proficient in it, and take a particular job related to it. Is this inner desire evidence that it is God's will that we go into a specific career?

In addition to making the choice of a career, we also look for a companion. We look at many, meet some, date a few of these, develop close relationships with a handful, and eventually focus time and attention on one. As we grow in our relationship with this particular one, we begin to feel that inner desire and compulsion to have that person as our partner for life. Is this strong desire to marry that person a sign that it is God's will?

79

The way God works

Could this be God at work in the believer? Could He be giving us inner desires to move into a certain vocation or marry a certain person? Philippians 2:12, 13 is an instructive portion of the Word to deal with this question:

> So then, my beloved, just as you have always obeyed, not as in my presence only, but now much more in my absence, work out your salvation with fear and trembling; for it is God who is at work in you, both to will and to work for His good pleasure.

Verse 12 presents the human side of the Christian life. The believer is to work out his salvation, which in this particular case refers to the corporate spiritual life of the church at Philippi. Christians are to accomplish this task with an attitude of fear and trembling toward each other. Verse 13 presents the explanation of how this takes place. It is the power of God at work in the believers. He is active in them and His activity is described by two verbs — *to will* and *to work*. God implants in His people the *desire* or *wish* to do His will as well as the *energy* or *impetus* to actually accomplish the work. When I feel an inclination to say something or do something or go somewhere and if this inclination is in accord with the Word of God, then it fits with Philippians 2:13 — God is at work in me producing the inclination. The latter part of verse 13 shows us that this God-given inner desire will always be directed toward His good pleasure, another way of referring to His will. So my inner inclination may well have a divine source — God. He is at work, prompting me to think and act in certain specific ways.

This ministry is carried on in the believer by the indwelling Holy Spirit. Romans 8:14 concludes that one of the basic marks of our spiritual sonship is the reality of "being led by the Spirit of God." An example of this occurred when Philip was led by the Spirit to witness to the Ethiopian eunuch (Acts 8:29). The Holy Spirit prompted Peter's positive response to the three men sent to him by Cornelius (Acts 10:19, 20). The leaders of the church at Antioch sent Paul and Barnabas on their first missionary journey as a result of being sensitive to the word of the Spirit to them (Acts 13:2). Paul and Silas took a detour on one of their missionary treks as a result of the Spirit's suggestion (Acts 16:6). Later, Paul told the elders of the church at Ephesus that the Spirit who was leading him to go to Jerusalem had also impressed upon him the fact that bonds and afflictions awaited him (Acts 20:22, 23). Apparently the Spirit spoke audibly to some of the early Christian leaders to lead them to do the will of God, but that was prior to the completion of the New Testament. Now with a completed, authoritative revelation of the will of God, the Spirit has His sword — the Word of God — and uses it to lead us. The inner drives and desires we experience will never be contrary to the Word and must always be tested by the Word.

So we see that God doesn't leave us with a will that is neutral, vacillating in the winds of our emotions and intellect. He works in us both to desire certain things and to do them.

The compelling desire to study medicine or law or theology can well be God's work in us. The strong inclination to marry Sue or Sam or to remain single could also be God at work in a person.

Guidelines

God will not give us desires contrary to His Word. We may have them, but they are not from God. You may have a strong desire to marry Charlie, but he is not a Christian. So rest assured it is not God at work in you, because His good pleasure is that you marry a believer. Suppose a Christian fellow has a strong desire to marry a girl who is also a Christian, but she doesn't have that same compulsion. They had better wait until she gets it or he loses it! God could work either direction.

As a rule, God won't give us desires contrary to common sense. You want to marry a person you have known for two months. That doesn't make sense. You cannot get to know a person well enough in so short a period of time to know whether you really want to commit yourself to him or her for a lifetime relationship. You want to quit your job and go into business for yourself. With a new baby, a small bank account, and lots of debts — that doesn't make sense, right now.

In the same way, God does not normally give us an inner compulsion that is opposed to circumstantial evidence and the counsel of others. You may want to go into art or architecture, but if you are not able to draw or design and your friends advise against it, then chances are the desire is not from God.

Sometimes we feel strong inclinations to do things that are wrong. The desire may be so intense that we fail to evaluate it carefully and we succumb to the pressure of the moment. This is certainly not God at work in us. It is the flesh setting its desire against that of the Spirit (Gal. 5:17). We may go into a store to shop and experience that strong desire to buy something we do not need or into a restaurant and have that inner compulsion to eat too much. If we do not have the money and do not need the food, the pressure is not being applied by God. We experience a lot of internal proddings to act and react in ways that are not in the will of God. We feel compelled to blame our mate for our own shortcomings. We are tempted to compare our children with each other. Teenagers feel a strong inclination to rebel against the authority of their parents, the school, and the state. Sometimes we have the urge to tell somebody exactly what we think of them. Normally this would not be God at work in us. It is the action or response of a self-centered person who is not being prompted by God at all. The Word of God is the key. Check all desires and inclinations by the standard of the Word. If they square with the Word, they could be from God. Or if they are not in any way opposed to the Word, they could be from God. It is imperative that the believer know the Word.

12

Contentment and the Will of God

The way God works

God does not want confused, bewildered, frustrated Christians wandering around anxiously searching for His will. He wants people who are walking confidently and peacefully in His will. Along with an inner compulsion there should be an inner contentment — a feeling and a conviction that a certain choice or act is the right thing to do. There should be no doubts and uncertainties and there should be a sense of peace and contentment that a given decision is precisely what God wants us to do.

In Colossians 3:15 Paul exhorts believers to "let the peace of Christ rule in your hearts. . . ." The word "peace" means a state of harmony and inner tranquillity. It is that feeling we have when things are all right. Paul says that this feeling of inner tranquillity is to "rule" in our hearts. This word "rule" refers to the activity of the umpire at an athletic contest. He makes the decisions. He settles the disputes. Peace is to play the role of an umpire in our lives. Peace renders the decisions. Peace settles the disputes.

The words of Colossians 3:15 were written to a group of believers who were seeking to get along with each other in harmony and unity. That was God's will for them and Paul gives them some specific directions about how to achieve it in verses 12 through 14. He tells them to be compassionate, kind, humble, gentle, and patient with each other. He encourages them to work at learning how to put up with one another and how to forgive one another and how to love one another. Then in verse 15 he tells them to use peace to test whether they are doing what they ought to be doing. He might have written something like this:

"Did you really forgive that brother?"

"I think so."

"How do you feel about it?"

"Kind of uneasy — not too good, as a matter of fact."

"Then you don't have peace. You better go to him and work it out. Then you'll have a feeling of contentment that will let you know that you're in God's will."

If a group of believers are to know and do the will of God, they must have attitudes and actions that are governed by their emotional umpire — peace. What is true interpersonally is also true intrapersonally. That is, within each individual believer peace can function as a God-given umpire to let us know that our attitudes and actions are those with which God is pleased.

God has made us — emotions and all. It makes sense that actions in harmony with His will would produce feelings in us that are positive. The person who avoids the wicked and the sinful and delights in the law of the Lord will be happy (Ps. 1:1, 2). The Lord gave His disciples commandments to be understood and acted upon so that their "joy may be made full" (John 15:10, 11). In fact, the one who lives in the presence of God is promised "fulness of joy" (Ps. 16:11). Feelings of peace and contentment are available to help us call the decisions of life according to the will of God.

The alternatives

Examining some of the alternatives mentioned in Scripture will help us to understand the concept of contentment better. The first is *confusion*. First Corinthians 14:33 states that "God is not a God of confusion but of peace, as in all the churches of the saints." The Corinthians were out of the will of God in many areas, especially with regard to spiritual gifts. Any congregation out of the will of God will be characterized by confusion. James uses this same word when he writes, "For where jealousy and selfish ambition exist, there is *disorder* and every evil thing" (James 3:16). It never fails; jealousy and selfish ambition among believers will produce disorder and all of this will be a clear indication that the congregation is not functioning according to the will of God.

What is true of a congregation is also true of an individual. When I am unsettled and confused about a matter instead of peacefully sublime, it is a good indication that either I have not yet discovered the will of God in that matter or the route I am going is not His will. For example, in a marriage where the husband is a weak leader, or in a family where the parents are very lenient with the children, all of the parties involved will at times feel a sense of confusion. That is because they are not operating on biblical standards.

When the believer is aware of what God wants him to be and do and yet does not consistently function in this way, he is living with an unsettling ambivalence — created by the pull of God's will in one direction and his own will in the other direction. The Bible describes this person as "double-minded" and then goes on to characterize him as "unstable in all his ways" (James 1:8). The Greek word for "unstable" is the same one that Paul uses in 1 Corinthians 14:33 ("confusion") and that James uses again in 3:16 ("disorder"). The New Testament teaches that when we are out of God's will, we are an unsettled, confused group of believers and we feel it similarly in our own individual hearts.

85

Anxiety is another alternative to peace. Philippians 4:6, 7 deals with this issue:

> Be anxious for nothing, but in everything by prayer and supplication with thanksgiving let your requests be made known to God. And the peace of God, which surpasses all comprehension, shall guard your hearts and your minds in Christ Jesus.

Christians are not to be tense and uptight. When we are submerged in worry and anxiety, we are out of the will of God. How do we handle our anxieties? We talk to God about them. We tell Him exactly what it is that is bothering us. We let Him know how we feel and why we feel as we do. We do all this with thanksgiving. God forces us to balance all of our negative feelings with the positive attitude of thanks for the situation. When we communicate with God openly about our anxieties, we will receive the promise of verse 7 — peace. Such a state of being is not only the absence of frustrating anxiety but also the presence of that emotional state that will enable us to continue to discover the will of God. An anxious Christian has trouble finding the will of God, not only because the anxiety itself has him out of the will of God but also because his emotional state is such that he cannot even get hold of the peace he needs to test other aspects of God's will for him. It is harder to play the game when the umpire is not even on the field! These verses also underscore the importance of prayer in discovering the will of God. If I am concerned about whether to take a job with another company, I should openly and honestly share all the details of my concern about this decision with God. When I do this, God will give me peace. Peace is the context for me to then determine what God wants me to do.

We often hear people say, "I don't have peace about this matter yet." They are on solid biblical ground. It is right to look for a feeling of peace about a decision and when we have that feeling of peace, it is one good way of knowing we are in God's will.

Physical and emotional distress is another alternative to peace. David went through a long period of time when he was out of the will of God in terms of a failure to confess his sin. He reveals in Psalm 32:3, 4 that he was miserable during that time: "When I kept silent about my sin, my body wasted away through my groaning all day long." Unconfessed sin produced physical suffering so penetrating that his bones hurt, so painful that he groaned. "For day and night Thy hand was heavy upon me . . . ." He remained in a continual state of depression, even recognizing that it was the hand of God creating the pressure on his soul. When we fail to deal openly and honestly with sin in our lives, we endure the same kind of distress, both physically and psychologically. But when we confront the sin in our lives and confess it, we experience the joy of fellowship with God and others (1 John 1:4). Confession brings peace — a peace that testifies to us that we are where God wants us to be.

This does not mean that every ulcer or headache is a signal that we are out of God's will, nor that all feelings of depression are indicators of disobedience. But it does mean that when we are distressed, physically or emotionally, we should evaluate where we are in relation to God's truth. The lack of peace could be a warning to us that instead of being transformed by the truth, we are still being conformed to the world. On occasions when I have trouble going to sleep or wake up early and can't get back to sleep, I have found it profitable to take stock of my relationship to my Lord and to significant others in my life. Inability to sleep is very distressing to me and I find I sleep best when I'm peaceful.

Doubting is another alternative to peace. Romans 14:22, 23 says, "Happy is he who does not condemn himself in what he approves. But he who doubts is condemned if he eats, because his eating is not from faith; and whatever is not from faith is sin." The believer is to have thoroughgoing convictions about any particular course of action he intends to take, especially in that gray area of questionable practices. When he experiences self-condemnation or personal doubts about his actions, those feelings of doubts should alert him to the fact that this may not be the will of God. A settled certainty is the kind of noncondemning contentment we can have when we are doing what God wants us to do. That uneasy, unsettled, wavering feeling is something God says we should be sensitive to. On occasion, after I fire a witty, off-the-cuff remark at a friend, I reflect on what I've said, and then those unsettling doubts tell me that it was not clever wit; it was really caustic sarcasm — words not spoken according to the will of God. There are times when our family is watching a television program that I will feel doubts as to the wisdom of exposing ourselves to such ideas and innuendos — doubts that are simply alerting me to the will of God.

Confusion, anxiety, physical distress, and doubts are some of the inadequate alternatives to peace. A lack of contentment will usually mean that one of the above will be present instead. When they are, we need to get more insight from the Word and other believers.

Careers and companions

In reference to a choice of a personal vocation, we have indicated that God can work in us to want to pursue a particular career. But along with this inner compulsion we should check out the matter of contentment. Maybe the career you are interested in involves selling and traveling, yet it is not only painful for you to close a deal but you get homesick even at a slumber party across town! This could be a way of sensing it is not God's will for you. Your interest may involve designing machines to do certain things and this gives you immense feelings of personal satisfaction; quite possibly this is an indication of God's will. It may involve working in a large company where you will never be your own boss and you know you will chafe under this; in such a situation you would be anything but content. It could be that it is not His will. Perhaps you have in mind studying and communicating the Word of God to people. The very thought of doing this makes you feel thrilled and excited. Such positive feelings may be a good indication that God's will for you is some kind of Christian ministry.

In the matter of choosing a life's mate, feelings are definitely involved. If you and the person you are dating differ drastically in basic areas such as future plans, values, money, etc., then you probably have some real doubts about the relationship. Where there are doubts, there is no contentment and where there is no real contentment, you have not yet found the right person. Perhaps your current companion frequently loses his or her temper or he says he loves you but seldom demonstrates it. It is hard to be content with such a relationship. God has something better in store for you. On the other hand, when you love each other and can argue constructively, each one willing to give and bend and to accept minor differences, and when you are both committed to the Lord and are both aiming at the same life goals, you have so much going for you that there will be a real sense of contentment and peace. This is a positive emotional endorsement by the Spirit of God that you are in the will of God.

A personal illustration

At the beginning of my senior year in college I was growing steadily in my relationship with a pretty young lady named Audrey. I felt both an inner compulsion and an inner contentment about asking her to be my wife. I did so and she indicated that she felt the same and so we became engaged. At the time I was majoring in business administration and, though not too highly motivated in any vocational direction, I assumed I would return to my home in Tucson, Arizona, and go into business with my father. During that year I began to note a slow but definite interest in going into the ministry. This was so foreign to anything I had ever contemplated before that I paid little attention to it, but it kept increasing in intensity. By the time graduation from college rolled around, I felt a strong inner compulsion to go to seminary and study for the ministry. Right after graduation I received a notice from the draft board inviting me to appear for induction into the armed forces. It seemed that they needed me to help in the Korean War, which was in full swing at the time. Suddenly I noticed an intense increase in my desire to go into the ministry. That was because if I went to seminary I would be exempt from the draft. But I checked my feelings. I was high on compulsion and low on contentment. I didn't feel real peace about going to seminary. I sensed that at that point in my life the motive was primarily to avoid the draft; thus I had no peace about the decision. So I joined the navy (rather than being drafted into the army) and spent the next four years allowing God to solidly confirm in my mind that I was to go to seminary and prepare for the ministry of the Word. I entered the navy in 1951 somewhat undecided about my vocational goal. I got out of the navy in 1955 thoroughly convinced that seminary was for me and completely content about the decision. I have never had second thoughts about that decision. For me it was the will of God, confirmed personally by a deep personal desire to go into the ministry and further confirmed by a real feeling of personal contentment about the choice.

Audrey's and my earlier compulsion and contentment about the decision to marry had long before led to our marriage. We were married two weeks before I entered the navy and so we had four years to adjust to each other and develop our relationship prior to my entering seminary.

A word of caution

Our feelings are strong and sometimes unstable. We can develop feelings of contentment about many things. Our emotions can short-circuit our thoughts and we can convince ourselves that a certain action is what we ought to do. So once again we need a standard and a guide. The Word is the answer. I must constantly check my emotions with the Word of God. God will never give me contentment about doing something opposed to His Word. If I have peace about an issue and yet I am basically at odds with the Word, then it is not His peace.

13

Suppose I Don't Do the Will of God

God has a desired will for each believer's life. He wants us to know and to do it. We have talked about how we can know it so that we can do it. We have accentuated the positive in the hopes of eliminating the negative. But we are imperfect human beings who will fail to do the will of God consistently. For a moment we need to elaborate on the negative.

Suppose a believer does not do the will of God. What happens? As in every area of life, when you do not abide by the rules, you pay the consequences. What are the consequences when we fail to do the will of God?

There may be pleasant consequences

When you conform to the language and action of a certain group, you normally feel good and accepted; perhaps you even become the leader — all pleasant consequences. Mary cheats on an exam and as a result gets a high grade — a pleasant consequence. Tom disobeys his parents by going somewhere he was not supposed to go and staying longer than he should have; but he had lots of fun — pleasant consequences. Shirley took credit for something she really didn't do and was applauded for it — pleasant consequences. You buy what you can't afford and go home with such a feeling of excitement with your new furniture. You eat more than you should; it's bad for your health, but right now you have that pleasant, full feeling. You neglect your wife and children in order to make more money and bring home a bigger paycheck — more money is a pleasant consequence.

All of these examples support the simple fact that you can be out of the will of God and still experience pleasant consequences. They may be very temporary or they may last a long time. The use of drugs gives one a pleasant "high" that is short-lived. On the other hand, a stolen Honda may provide for its new owner many months and miles of pleasant travel.

Sin can be fun. Hebrews 11:25 comments on this fact in referring to Moses as one who chose to endure ill-treatment with the people of God rather than enjoy the passing pleasures of sin. The pleasures that Moses gave up are referred to in 11:24 and 26. He refused to be called the son of Pharaoh's daughter and, as a result, to have at his disposal the treasures of Egypt. Status and money are two highly desirable commodities that everyone wants. Sin can be pleasant; make no mistake about it. If it were not, we wouldn't have such a problem with it. But Satan is a deceiver (Rev. 12:9) and a master of disguise (2 Cor. 11:14); he makes the bad appear good. This is one of his basic schemes (cf. Eph. 6:11). Therefore you can be out of the will of God and still be enjoying life, happy and carefree, with things seemingly going your way.

I asked my barber why no one had yet discovered a cure for baldness. His reply made good sense. He said, "Because there is no pain with baldness. If it hurt to be bald, then we would be hard at work on the solution." Why is it that people are not greatly concerned about being out of the will of God? It could be that right now they are having too much fun. They are experiencing pleasure; they are not looking for relief from pain. So we are often deceived by the presence of pleasant feelings and pleasant consequences, because there can be pleasure in sin.

There will be unpleasant consequences

While it is true that there *may be* pleasant consequences when we do not do the will of God, it is also true that there *will be* unpleasant consequences. The pleasure of sin is a passing thing. The justice of God is not. Woven into the fabric of His world is God's "if — then" formula. You can see it in 1 Kings 9. It is stated positively in verses 4 and 5: "If you will walk before Me . . . in integrity of heart and uprightness . . . *then* I will establish the throne of your kingdom forever . . . ." In the next two verses it is stated negatively: "But *if* you . . . turn away from following Me . . . *then* I will cut off Israel from the land which I have given them. . . ." Deuteronomy 28 sets forth the same formula with explicit details. Obey and I will bless you (vv. 1-14). Disobey and I will curse you (vv. 15-68). A familiar passage in Numbers reiterates the same principle: "But if you will not do so, behold, you have sinned against the Lord, and be sure your sin will find you out" (32:23).

This principle of consequences is also clearly established in the New Testament in Galatians 6:6-8:

> And let the one who is taught the word share all good things with him who teaches. Do not be deceived, God is not mocked; for whatever a man sows, this he will also reap. For the one who sows to his own flesh shall from the flesh reap corruption, but the one who sows to the Spirit shall from the Spirit reap eternal life.

In verse 6 there is an exhortation to the pupil to remunerate his teacher with all things (both spiritual and material). Since it is easy for believers to present a facade and pretend they are doing this, Paul injects a clear, concise principle in verse 7: You may be superficial in your support, but God knows what is going on and you will reap what you sow. God is not mocked. To mock God is literally "to turn up the nose" at God. One does not do this without paying the consequences. If believers are unreceptive and unappreciative of spiritual teaching, this is

93

probably a specific example of their attitude toward life in general. But one cannot outwit God. It is vain to expect to reap a harvest different from what has been sown. When one sows to his own flesh (sin), he will reap corruption from the flesh (unpleasant consequences) (v. 8). This is a principle and a warning. When one violates the known will of God, he will and he must pay the consequences.

The consequences are characterized as *unpleasant* because that is precisely the way the Word of God refers to them: "All discipline for the moment seems not to be joyful, but sorrowful . . ." (Heb. 12:11). This is how God works in the believer's life. The disobedient believer is not being punished as an unforgiven sinner, he is being disciplined as a wayward saint. Proverbs 3:11, 12; John 15:2; and Revelation 3:19 all refer to the activity of God in the Christian whereby He brings jarring experiences to straighten him out. When the believer gets out of the will of God, regardless of how pleasant it may seem initially, eventually he will come under the discipline of God. It will inevitably happen, because the Lord loves all of his children and "whom the Lord loves he disciplines" (Heb. 12:6).

Kinds of unpleasant consequences

There are the *natural effects* of our bad behavior. When we don't eat the right foods or get the proper rest and exercise, we have physical problems. Drinking and drugs can affect us physically, mentally, and emotionally, even to the point of addiction. When we keep to ourselves things that ought to be shared with others, we suffer the emotional problems that go with suppression. Seldom do we suffer alone. Our sin has secondhand consequences in the lives of others. Lost jobs, broken homes, ruptured relationships, automobile accidents, and other misfortunes affect many others besides ourselves. God has built into His world cause-and-effect relationships — natural consequences that will inevitably take place. When we violate these natural laws or seek to outwit them, we pay the consequences. The Word does not give us much revelation about the natural effects of bad behavior; it majors on what *is* bad behavior. But experience tells us much about it and we have seen from our study of common sense that God expects us to learn from our experience.

There are *feelings of guilt*, which are unpleasant. Sometimes these feelings are unnecessary. If they are produced by a nonbiblical legalism or a failure to realize that one is righteous (not guilty) in Christ, then the person is doing battle with unnecessary feelings. But if the believer has chosen consciously and willfully to violate truth that he understands, then he will feel bad. If he doesn't, he ought to, as James says, "Be miserable and mourn and weep: let your laughter be turned into mourning, and your joy to gloom" (James 4:9). This is the constructive sorrow that results in repentance. Paul speaks of it in 2 Corinthians 7:9, 10.

We have seen from the experience of David in Psalm 32 that guilt feelings can be extremely unpleasant. The United States Internal Revenue Service can attest to the same fact, since that office receives thousands of dollars every year from citizens who cheated on their income tax returns in the past and cannot live with their guilt feelings any longer.

For the Christian it is the Word of God applied by the Spirit of God that is making him aware of what is wrong in his life. Ephesians 6:17 indicates that the sword of the Spirit is the Word of God and 2 Timothy 3:16 informs us that the Word is profitable for both reproof and correction. Thus, when we have violated God's Word, He makes us aware of this fact, and the awareness carries with it the unpleasant consequences of guilt feelings. The only way to deal with these adequately is by confession — to God and man.

There are the direct *interventions* of God to discipline us. This subject is treated with detail in 1 Corinthians 11:27-32. First, there is the exhortation in verse 28 that every believer is to conduct a personal, self-examination of his own life. The Greek word translated "examine" is the same as that used in Romans 12:2 of the believer's work of proving or testing to discover the will of God. Here it is a healthy internal examination that is to be carried on prior to participating in the Lord's Supper. The next four verses develop the concept that if we don't examine ourselves and make the changes that need to be made, God will do it for us. He will examine us, and where we need discipline, He will administer it. Evidence of His hand of discipline is given in verse 30: "For this reason [the lack of self-examination] many among you are weak and sick, and a number sleep." God has invaded this group of sinning, unrepentant believers and brought physical discipline into their lives for being and remaining out of the will of God.

Ananias and Sapphira tried to lie to the leaders of the church in Jerusalem about their finances and God brought swift judgment upon them in the form of death (Acts 5:1-11). Apparently the early church needed such drastic purifying action as seen in Jerusalem and Corinth to impress on them the nature of the holiness and justice of God as well as the need for personal purity in the believer's life. Though it does not appear that God has continued to intervene in believers' lives with the same kind of immediate, drastic action, we have seen earlier that God is very much involved in all of the circumstances of our lives (Eccl. 7:13, 14; Rom. 8:28). These circumstances may be to discipline us, and they can be painful (Heb. 12:5-11). The sensitive believer should analyze the unpleasant, trying situations of his life to see if and how the disciplinary activity of God is at work in his own experience to cause him to know and do the will of God.

One other unpleasant consequence is that of the *confrontation* of other believers. This process is clearly outlined in Matthew 18:15-17:

> And if your brother sins, go and reprove him in private; if he listens to you, you have won your brother. But if he does not listen to you, take one or two more with you, so that by the mouth of two or three witnesses every fact may be confirmed. And if he refuses to listen to them, tell it to the church; and if he refuses to listen even to the church, let him be to you as a Gentile and a tax-gatherer.

Note that the focus is on a brother who sins, that is, a believer out of the will of God. He is to be dealt with in a series of confrontations. First, he is to be reproved in private (v. 15). If this is not successful, then two or three believers are to confront him (v. 16). If this fails to yield results, the matter is to be brought before the entire church; if he remains unrepentant, he is to be excluded from fellowship (v. 17).

This whole process can be most unpleasant for the sinning brother as well as the others who are involved, but it is God's way of handling His disobedient children. Other passages dealing with this same topic of church discipline are 1 Corinthians 5; 2 Corinthians 2; 2 Thessalonians 3:14, 15; and Titus 3:10. Churches that consistently apply these principles are churches where the members are impressed with the importance of knowing and doing God's will. Where confrontation is spasmodic and crisis-oriented believers are often satisfied with mediocrity in terms of the will of God.

To gain additional insight on this process one should study the significant biblical word "admonition," the translation of a Greek word meaning "to have a corrective influence on someone." This was so vital a part of Paul's ministry that he even goes so far as to say that the two basic factors involved in bringing a believer to maturity are *admonishing* and *teaching* (Col. 1:28). In the same letter he tells the entire church that as the Word richly indwells them, they should engage in the same two-pronged ministry of "teaching and admonishing one another" (Col. 3:16). Other instructive occurrences of the word are in Acts 20:31; Romans 15:14; 1 Corinthians 4:14; and 1 Thessalonians 5:12.

We would like to find a way to grow without having any unpleasant experiences. It doesn't happen that way. All maturing growth involves both the pleasant and the painful. Believers help one another grow through a process that involves confronting in order to correct. That isn't always pleasant but it is profitable. Frequently we protect our friends from the truth about themselves and about the will of God out of a mistaken notion that it is more important that they *feel* good than that they *be* good. One thing that God has done to keep us in His will is to authorize other believers to call our attention to the fact that we are not.

Our reaction to the unpleasant consequences

How should we who are Christians react to the unpleasant consequences of being out of God's will? We should face the facts! We should openly and honestly evaluate what is going on in our own personal lives. If we are out of the will of God, we must admit it and deal with it. If God is to bring conviction through discipline, we ought to respond in a healthy, biblical way. This means being "sorrowful to the point of repentance" (cf. 2 Cor. 7:9, 10). That is constructive sorrow — sorrow that is according to the will of God and produces a repentance without regret. This constructive sorrow and repentance includes the process of self-examination and self-judgment outlined in 1 Corinthians 11:27-32 and confession to God and to any others significantly involved (James 5:16; 1 John 1:9).

David spent nearly a year feeling miserably guilty about his sin. He had committed adultery and then murder, and on those two counts he was out of the will of God. He suffered the consequences by being physically, emotionally, and spiritually miserable (Ps. 32:3, 4). Finally, he faced the issues squarely and dealt with them by open and honest confession to God (Ps. 32:5; 51:1-4). He then experienced the happiness of the man "in whose spirit there is no deceit!" (Ps. 32:2). He experienced the sense of forgiveness that comes when we wholeheartedly agree with God's view of our life situation. Unpleasant circumstances ought to drive us to God rather than to despair. So the issue is not whether we will have unpleasant consequences — we will. The issue is how we will react to them.

The results

Unpleasant circumstances are designed to produce results in our lives. Just as human discipline is to produce maturity, so also is divine discipline. In Hebrews 12:10 God is said to discipline us "for our good, that we may share His holiness." In verse 11 the writer goes on to say that those who have been trained by divine discipline will evidence the peaceful fruit of righteousness. When we react properly to discipline, we grow. In 2 Corinthians 7:11 Paul outlines the positive results that godly sorrow has accomplished in the lives of the Corinthian Christians. He uses words such as "earnestness," "longing," and "zeal." Repentance involved a healthy behavioral change in their lives. That's practical holiness.

God wants us to do His will. He has given us a revelation of it in His Word. When we do not do it, we experience the consequences, which, though they may be pleasant for a time, eventually will include the unpleasant. God designs the unpleasantness to awaken, convict, instruct, and admonish us. He may do this to remind us of what we already know or to teach us what we need to know. To respond with hostility or indifference is to miss the opportunity to grow in our understanding of the will of God.

14

Questions About the Will of God

1. *Suppose a Christian who is aware of 2 Corinthians 6:14-18 marries an unbeliever. Is he out of the will of God for the rest of his married life with regard to this issue?*

Only as long as it is an unresolved issue in the life of the believer. When he faces it and deals with it with godly sorrow and repentance (2 Cor. 7:7-11; James 4:8-10) and makes confession to those persons directly involved (James 5:16; 1 John 1:9), he will experience the joy of forgiveness and fellowship. From that point he can go on to live as God wants him to in a mixed marriage, seeking to attract his mate to Christ (1 Cor. 7:12-16; 1 Peter 3:1-7).

2. *Can I be in the will of God and not know it?*

Yes. We can say and do certain things that are in harmony with the Word of God and yet not be consciously aware of the fact that we are putting the Word into effect in our lives. However, this is not living at the level God expects of us. for He wants us to be filled with the *knowledge* of His will (Col. 1:9) and to *consciously do* all to His glory (1 Cor. 10:31).

3. Can certain aspects of the will of God become habitual in our lives so that we do them automatically?

Certainly. God has made us as creatures of habit and we can train and discipline ourselves to do consistently specific things that are in harmony with His will; e.g., matters of courtesy, habits of health and cleanliness, ways of reacting to stress, etc. One problem with the consistent repetition of an attitude or action is that though it may outwardly appear to be a habit of holiness, it may inwardly degenerate to sterile ritual that the Lord condemns as hypocritical (Matt. 15:1-9; 23:1-39). The will of God is to be done from the heart (Eph. 6:6); that is, it should spring from an internal motivation to serve and please God rather than to perform for men. The Christian should test his habit patterns (like going to church and saying grace) with the question "Am I consciously doing this to glorify God?"

One further word needs to be said. Though we are creatures of habit, we are *sinful* creatures of habit, and our habits operate in the context of a heart that is deceitful and desperately sick (Jer. 17:9) — a heart that can produce all kinds of evil (Matt. 15:17-20) and is subject to all kinds of temptations (1 Cor. 10:13). Even as we develop good, God-honoring habits, we must remain alert. "Let him who thinks he stands take heed lest he fall" (1 Cor. 10:12).

4. Is it the will of God that I marry one specific person?

Yes and no. Yes, with regard to God's determined will. If you marry, you *will* marry the person God sovereignly planned for you to marry. No, with regard to God's desired will. His desired will is that you marry a believer with whom you can develop a relationship that is in harmony with all that the Word of God says about marriage and the family. This person could conceivably be any one of a number of men or women. As in other areas, your responsibility is to "understand what the will of the Lord is" (Eph. 5:17) in the matter of a marriage partner. You do this by developing relationships with members of the opposite sex, looking for that person with whom you can best put into effect the biblical roles and responsibilities of being partners and parents.

5. *Do we ever mature to the point where our will is the same as God's will?*

Not in this life. That implies perfection and only in heaven will we be perfect. We do, however, reach a point where we are "trained to discern good and evil" (Heb. 5:14). This is the mark of maturity. The Bible paradoxically says that this maturity is something we *reach* and yet something we are always *reaching for.* Paul classified certain of the Philippian Christians as being already perfect (mature, Phil. 3:15), yet in the same context he spoke of the fact that he himself was continuing to reach forward for this same perfection (maturity, Phil. 3:12, 13).

6. *Can believers be out of the will of God and not know it?*

Yes, but the fact that they do not know it means that they are ignorantly rather than willfully failing to accomplish God's will. "To one who knows the right thing to do, and does not do it, to him it is sin" (James 4:17). When I fail to act on what I know, I am sinning. When I fail to act on what I don't know, I am not consciously sinning, though I may still suffer many of the consequences of the sinful act. A Christian couple may be ignorant of their biblical responsibility to discipline their children consistently. Failure to do this is not a willful, conscious sin on their part, but even so, they and their children will reap the consequences of the lack of consistent discipline.

It is also true that ignorance of the will of God may itself be sin, for the believer is to have an insatiable appetite for the Word and is to study it often in order to grow (1 Peter 2:2). When the opportunity to do this is present, and I fail to take advantage of it, I am out of God's will.

7. *Is being in the will of God the same as being in fellowship with God?*

Yes. These are two ways of looking at the same thing. A

believer who is "in fellowship with God" will be keeping His commandments, and a believer who is keeping His command-

nts will be doing God's will (cf. John 15:1-14; 1 John 1). The concept of living the Christian life is presented in many ways in the Bible: walking in .he Spirit, abiding in Christ, putting off the old man, putting on the new man, being edified, being filled with the Spirit, keeping the commandments, walking in the light, etc. These are all different sides of the same basic coin, each one amplifying and stressing a particular aspect of Christian growth and maturation.

8. Can I be out of the will of God in one area and in the will of God in another area at the same time?

Surely. You could conceivably witness to the bank teller while you are robbing the bank! Seriously, the will of God relates to the details of my life and I can be out of His will with regard to a certain detail and in His will with regard to some other detail. As a seminary professor, I may be in the will of God in terms of my preparation and presentation in a certain class and out of the will of God in terms of my relationship with a given student in that class. We can be obnoxious to fellow employees while we are being gracious to customers. Pastors can faithfully study and preach God's Word while they are failing to function biblically in their own home. God's Word is specific; therefore His will is specific. In Colossians 3:8, 9 we are told to put aside anger, wrath, malice, slander, abusive speech, and lying. In Colossians 3:12, 13 we are told to put on compassion, kindness, humility, gentleness, patience, forgiveness. These are specific qualities of life. When I put one of these into practice in my life, I am in the will of God with regard to that quality in that situation. However, the Word of God does not support "sectional sanctification." We may never be content to be spiritually "with it" in some areas and "out of it" in other areas. In fact, the Bible tells us not to offer a gift to God if our brother has something against us (Matt. 5:23, 24). The will of God is to become more and more a complete way of life for us.

104

Patience, for example, is to be something that permeates our life style — a fruit that the Spirit wants to produce in out total life in *every* situation. Paul's injunction to the *total person* is to "walk [live your life] in a manner worthy of the Lord, to please Him in *all* respects, bearing fruit in *every* good work" (Col. 1:10).

9. *How does timing fit in with the will of God?*

We constantly face questions like the following: When should I take my vacation? When should I quit my job? How long should I live with my parents? When should we move to a larger house? When is the letter going to come? When should I buy a new car? When will I get relief from this pain? When should I get married? When should I share Christ with my friend? When should we start our family? How long should I put up with this situation?

God's Word tells us *what* He wants us to do, but does it tell us *when* we are to do it? One basic thrust of the Word is that we are to put the precepts and principles of the Word into effect *now*. *Now* is the day of salvation (2 Cor. 6:2). *Now* is the time to love my neighbor (Rom 13:8-14). *Now* is the time for me to be ashamed of the things I did before I was saved (Rom. 6:21). *Now* is the time to hunger and thirst for righteousness (Luke 6:21; cf. Matt. 5:6). So concerning those issues on which the Word has spoken, our primary responsibility it to *act now*. When should I share Christ with my friend? *Now!* When should I love my brother? *Now!* When should I obey my parents? *Now!* When should I write that letter admitting it was my fault? *Now!*

Another basic thrust of Scripture is that the Christian is to view time as *opportunity* (Greek, *kairos*) rather than *chronology* (Greek, *chronos*). It is "opportunity time" the believer is to be "making the most of" (redeeming) as he understands and does the will of God (Eph. 5:15-17; cf. Gal. 6:10; Col. 4:5). Thus, every life situation is to be viewed as an opportunity to do the will of God.

The focus of the Word is on *what, why,* and *how* I do

something rather than on *when* I do it. *What* I do on my vacation is a more crucial question than *when* I take it, because it is a time to be redeemed regardless of when I take it. *Why* I quit my job is a more significant question than *when* I quit it, because it was a decision that should have been made in the context of biblical principles, whenever it took place.

When time is viewed as "opportunity," it is obvious that certain times are more "opportune" than others for us to do things. For a family there is a time that is more opportune than any other for them to take their vacation and so to decide to take it at that time and use that time profitably is to be in God's will. When should I get married? Well, first determine if you want to get married right now. Perhaps school, travel, work, etc., are opportunities you wish to make the most of before you marry. But if you are ready now, first find the right person. Then the two of you should decide when would be the most opportune time for all those who are significantly involved and that will normally narrow it down to a particular date on the calendar. If you have not known each other long, or have not had much quality time together as yet, you will feed also that data into your decision-making process.

When will you get relief from your pain? Maybe next week. Maybe never. The only thing you know for sure about the will of God in the midst of pain is that His grace is sufficient to meet your need (2 Cor. 12:7-9; Phil. 4:19). Your responsibility is to seize the opportunity now to put that aspect of His will into effect in your life.

God's determined will for our lives is on a fixed time schedule, but we don't know what that schedule is and His Word doesn't reveal it to us (Eccl. 3:1-11). His desired will *is* revealed to us and our task is to respond to our time and to time our responses in such a way that we adequately use the opportunity to fulfill our biblical responsibility accurately.

10. *What about location and the will of God? Should I go away to college? Should I spend the summer at camp? Should we*

move to another state? Should I get my own apartment? Should we live in a small town? Which mission field should I go to? On and on the geographically oriented questions go, raising in our minds a basic question: Does the God who tells us what to do, also tell us where to do it?

God certainly tells us where to go to preach the gospel — everywhere: Jerusalem, Judea, Samaria, and the remotest part of the earth (Acts 1:8). But how do I know if I personally should go to a remote location to preach? And if to a remote place, which one? The Word of God does not exempt any believer from preaching the gospel, nor does it exempt any believer from the exhortation to go into all the world. So each and every Christian must be willing and available to go anywhere to preach the gospel. From that point on, we should be sensitive to external circumstances and counsel, and to internal compulsion and contentment. If these line up in favor of a particular place, this is a good indication that God wants us there. The fact that our country is permeated with a gospel witness and other countries have little or no witness would perhaps alert us to a significant "opportunity" to go elsewhere to do God's will.

Apart from the responsibility to preach the gospel everywhere, the Bible doesn't tell the Christian where he is to work, play, study, worship, or live — geographically speaking. The emphasis in Scripture is on *what* a person does, rather than on *where* he does it. Therefore our reasons for remaining in an area or relocating can and ought to have biblical significance. If you have to move to a climate more favorable for your child's health, you will do it as a concerned, loving parent acting to meet the need of your child. That is a geographical move with biblical implications. If you transfer to a different college, you do it with purpose — to get better training, to study under a particular professor, to be with certain friends, or for some other reason, any or all of which can be related to your own personal growth. God is keenly interested in that, too. If you take a job with a different company in a small town, you may do it to allow yourself more time to discharge your biblical responsibilities to yourself and your family. On the other hand, you may not be happy in a given geographical location, and your tendency may be to blame the weather, the kind of people who live there, different cultural patterns, the distance from your own home, etc., for your unhappiness. But the Word says that all the ingredients of happiness are produced *in* us by the Holy Spirit (Gal. 5:22, 23) and that we are to learn to be content in our circumstances, though they may not be what we would regard as ideal (Phil. 4:11).

We are to be person-oriented rather than place-oriented. Paul had a person orientation as he traveled. He wrote to the believers in Rome that he wanted to come to see *them* "in order that I may impart some spiritual gift to you, that you may be established; that is, that I may be encouraged together with you, while among you, each of us by the other's faith, both yours and mine" (Rom. 1:11, 12). His motivation was interpersonal rather than geographical. The Lord made it clear that all of us should have the same orientation when He said that our responsibility is to love God above all and to love our neighbor as ourselves (Matt. 22:37-39). We are to discharge these responsibilities where we are now located and if we move (whatever the reason —job, health, school, retirement), we should assume that there will be significant opportunities to fulfill these responsibilities in our new location.

11. *What about vocation and the will of God?*

The Bible is not a vocational guidance handbook. It doesn't tell us what careers are right and what careers are wrong, nor what particular career each one should follow. It does give us guidance as to what activities and relationships are right and wrong. If you are contemplating being a bank robber, you should forget it, not because the Bible says, "Don't be a bank robber," but because it says we should not steal but should have a job where we work to support ourselves in such a way that we are behaving properly toward outsiders (Exod. 20:15; 1 Thess. 4:11, 12). We should evaluate any vocational preference we have in terms of whether it would cause us to engage in activities and/or relationships that the Word says are wrong.

The basic vocational guidance that the Word gives you as a believer is "to walk in a manner worthy of the calling with which you have been called" (Eph. 4:1). Every believer has this calling (vocation) along with the vocation he pursues to support himself and his family. No matter what business or profession you are in, you can walk worthy of your spiritual calling.

The Scriptures do not tell you *which* vocation to choose or even *how* to choose a vocation. You should evaluate your own interests and desires and talents, get plenty of counsel from others who are in the career(s) in which you are interested, be sensitive to circumstances (such as summer job openings, things you read, field trips, courses you take, and assignments and projects that highly motivate you), and be constantly checking out your own feelings to know what it is that really gives you a sense of purpose and fulfillment. God will work through all of these avenues to bring you to a knowledge of His will in the matter of a career.

What about going into full-time ministry? All of the instructions in the preceding paragraph apply, but along with these we have more detailed revelation in Scripture. The basic passage is 1 Timothy 3:1-7, with Titus 1:5-9 being a parallel passage on the same topic. Paul states that "if any man aspires to the office of overseer, it is a fine work he desires to do" (1 Tim. 3:1). Note that aspiration and desire can and should be present. One who is going into the ministry should *want very much* to do this. Also note that it is a "fine" work. The Greek word for "fine" means that which is "good, excellent, orderly, and right." The ministry is to be regarded as highly important, significant, and satisfying work. In 1 Timothy 3:2-7 are listed the qualifications for one who wants to serve in the ministry. They relate to all the various areas of one's character and conduct, public and private. A young person who feels led to go into the ministry should be developing a life style that is aimed in the direction of these

109

qualities. How can he determine if his life is moving in this direction? He should judiciously evaluate himself and also ask those who are spiritual leaders in the church to evaluate him in terms of these qualities. Timothy and Titus were made aware of these qualifications so that they could counsel and evaluate others who wanted to move into positions of spiritual leadership. If all the internal data and the external data is positive, you should seek opportunities to apprentice yourself to one who is already a spiritually mature leader and allow him to train you for an effective ministry. This procedure is clearly outlined in 2 Timothy 2:2, "And the things which you have heard from me in the presence of many witnesses, these entrust to faithful men, who will be able to teach others also." Such training ought to take place in the context of the local church and can be supplemented by attendance at a Bible college and/or seminary.

Should every young person expect to have confidently crystallized his vocational choice during high school or college days so he can move right into his career without any hesitation? Though it might be desirable to do so, some do and some do not. If it is laziness that causes me to work spasmodically, or if it is instability or lack of dependability that causes me to go from job to job, then I am clearly out of the will of God in certain areas of my personal life. But if it is a matter of honestly not being certain about what I want to do, then, rather than fret about it, I ought to redeem the time — investigating different opportunities and possibilities, constantly processing all the data I get to gain as much insight as I can as to what job will allow me to discover, develop, and fulfill the God-given abilities I have. By the same token , I see nothing wrong with a person's changing jobs, or even careers, during his working life. There are many, many vocations that one can engage in to the glory of God.

12. *Can another person tell me what God's will is for my life?*

Yes, because another person may know more precisely what the Word teaches about an issue you are facing. If he does, he may be able to tell you what God's will is for you. Believers are to do this for one another (Rom. 15:14; Gal. 6:1; Col. 3:16); parents are to do it for their children (Eph. 6:1-4; Col. 3:20); pastors are to do it for their people (2 Tim. 4:2; Heb. 13:7, 17); and older people are to do it for younger people (Titus 2:1-6).

In areas where the Word does not explicitly speak; e.g., areas of location, vocation, timing, etc., those who are older, more experienced, and more mature can offer counsel. This counsel can be of real help, but it should not be construed as authoritative, as a "thus-saith-the-Lord." As a matter of fact, it could well be advice sprinkled with bias, prejudice, ignorance, and unevaluated experience. God's desire is that we learn to utilize dependently the insights of other members of the body of Christ and at the same time to use independently the Word of God to discover the will of God.

15

Putting It All Together

Defining the will of God

We have seen that the "will of God" refers either to God's determined will or to His desired will. These two aspects can be compared in the following way:

THE WILL OF GOD

His Determined Will

He "works all things after the counsel of His will" (Eph. 1:11).

This is God's predetermined plan.

It is inevitable — that which will happen.

It relates to everything in the universe that will happen.

We can know all of the details after they have happened. We can predict only that which is revealed in Scripture.

It involves God's sovereignty and man's responsibility.

Its ultimate purpose is to glorify God.

His Desired Will

We are to "understand what the will of the Lord is" (Eph. 5:17).

This is God's desired plan.

It is desirable — that which He wants to happen. It may or may not happen.

It relates to personal salvation and the process of sanctification.

All we need to know to be saved and sanctified is revealed by precept and principle in Scripture.

It involves God's sovereignty and man's responsibility.

Its ultimate purpose is to glorify God.

God has revealed certain things to us about His *determined will*. The *reality* of it is clearly taught in Scripture. The *reason* for it — God's sovereignty — is also plainly set forth. The *result* of it — glory to God — is also seen in the Word. But the one aspect we all want to know more about — the *details* of it — are left for the most part among the secret things that belong to the Lord our God (Deut. 29:29). The *desired will* of God is not a secret. The details of His plan and program for our lives are clearly revealed in Scripture. We can know them and we should do them.

When you talk about "the will of God," be sure you know what you are referring to. When you say, "I'll see you next week, the Lord willing," you are referring to the determined will of God, and the statement is both accurate and appropriate (see James 4:13-16). Whether you will, in fact, see your friend next week is not revealed in the Word of God. You won't know whether it was part of God's plan for your life until you actually see him. If you do see him, it was God's will. If you don't, it wasn't.

You could also say, "I want the Lord's will to be done in our meeting next week." Now you are referring to the desired will of God and what you say and do prior to and during the meeting (if it takes place) can accomplish the will of God. It will, if the attitudes, actions, and decisions of you and those who meet with you are in harmony with the Word of God.

Discovering the will of God

The desired will of God is discovered in God's Word and in God's work. These two factors can be visualized in the following way:

114

THE DESIRED WILL OF GOD

It is discovered in the
Word of God —
its precepts,
its principles.

It is discovered in the
Work of God —
in the world (external) and
in the person (internal),
through
    circumstances,
    counsel,
    consequences,
    conscience,
    common sense,
    compulsion, and
    contentment.

This is the primary and
sufficient
revelation
of the will
of God for
the unbeliever
and the believer.

This is the secondary and
supplementary revelation of
the will of God.

The Word of God is our primary and sufficient revelation of the will of God. Its precepts and principles tell us what we need to know to be saved and to progress in sanctification. The Word provides the believer with a *complete* revelation of God's will — complete in the sense that every area of life is dealt with. It is *not comprehensive*, for not every detail of life is treated. It is, however, a revelation that will adequately equip us to ascertain God's will. A knowledge of the Scriptures is mandatory, then, for any person who is concerned about God's will. There are no shortcuts or substitutes. The Word is indispensible.

The God who has spoken in the Bible is also at work in a variety of ways in our individual lives and in our world. We have seen that He uses such things as circumstances, counsel from others, and the consequences of our actions to make us aware of His will. We have also studied how our mind, emotions, and will are involved in the process of discovering and doing what God wants. All of these factors are important but not infallible, and so we must constantly test the external and internal evidence to see if it is validated by the Word of God.

You can know the will of God for your life. It is not something vague and mysterious that you have to guess at or grope for. It is not something elusive that you must seek to capture and then hold on to. The will of God is simply that which God wants to happen in your life and He is so interested in your knowing it and doing it that He has revealed it for you in His Word. May you "be filled with the knowledge of His will in all spiritual wisdom and understanding . . ." (Col. 1:9).

One more thing. Remember that question? You ought to be able to answer it with biblical confidence.

Was it God's will for you to read this book?